THE fruit COOKBOOK

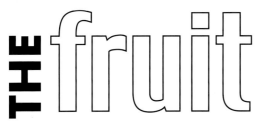

THE fruit
COOKBOOK

100 fresh and zesty recipes for desserts,
cakes, ices, salads, starters and main courses

**EMMA
SUMMER**

southwater

This edition is published by Southwater

Southwater is an imprint of Anness Publishing Ltd
Hermes House, 88–89 Blackfriars Road, London SE1 8HA
tel. 020 7401 2077; fax 020 7633 9499
www.southwaterbooks.com; info@anness.com

© Anness Publishing Ltd 1999, 2004

UK agent: The Manning Partnership Ltd, 6 The Old Dairy, Melcombe Road, Bath BA2 3LR;
tel. 01225 478444; fax 01225 478440; sales@manning-partnership.co.uk

UK distributor: Grantham Book Services Ltd, Isaac Newton Way, Alma Park Industrial Estate, Grantham, Lincs NG31 9SD;
tel. 01476 541080; fax 01476 541061; orders@gbs.tbs-ltd.co.uk

North American agent/distributor: National Book Network, 4501 Forbes Boulevard, Suite 200, Lanham, MD 20706;
tel. 301 459 3366; fax 301 429 5746; www.nbnbooks.com

Australian agent/distributor: Pan Macmillan Australia, Level 18, St Martins Tower, 31 Market St, Sydney, NSW 2000;
tel. 1300 135 113; fax 1300 135 103; customer.service@macmillan.com.au

New Zealand agent/distributor: David Bateman Ltd, 30 Tarndale Grove, Off Bush Road, Albany, Auckland; tel. (09) 415 7664; fax (09) 415 8892

Publisher Joanna Lorenz
Senior Cookery Editor Linda Fraser
Project Editor Emma Gray
Jacket Design Balley Design
Designers Lilian Lindblom, Bill Mason and Lisa Tai
Illustrations Anna Koska
Additional Text Christine Ingram

Photographers Karl Adamson, Edward Allwright, Steve Baxter, James Duncan, Michelle Garrett, Nelson Hargreaves,
Amanda Heywood, Tim Hill, David Jordan, Don Last, Patrick McLeavey, Michael Michaels, Thomas Odulate.
Recipes Alex Barker, Carla Capalbo, Kit Chan, Carole Clements, Roz Denny, Nicola Diggins, Rafi Fernandez, Christine France,
Sarah Gates, Shirley Gill, Rosamund Grant, Deh-Ta Hsiung, Patricia Lousada, Norma MacMillan, Sue Maggs, Sallie Morris,
Katherine Richmond, Anne Sheasby, Liz Trigg, Laura Washburn, Pamela Westland, Steven Wheeler, Elizabeth Wolf-Cohen.
Food for photography Madeleine Brehaut, Joanne Craig, Marilyn Forbes, Hilary Guy, Carole Handslip, Jane Hartshorn, Cara Hobday, Maria Kelly,
Wendy Lee, Blake Minton, Kirsty Rawlings, Jane Stevenson, Fiona Tillett, Judy Williams and Elizabeth Wolf-Cohen.

For all recipes, quantities are given in both metric and imperial measures and, where appropriate, measures are also given in
standard cups and spoons. Follow one set, but not a mixture, because they are not interchangeable.

1 3 5 7 9 10 8 6 4 2

contents

INTRODUCTION

There is nothing like the sight of a glorious display of fruit to lift the spirits and whet the appetite. Glowing colours, gorgeous scents and tastes that range from tantalisingly tart to superbly sweet – all these attributes help to make fruit the treat it undoubtedly is. Add the fact that it is a supremely healthy food, bursting with natural, energy-giving sugars, minerals and vitamins, in all the right quantities, and it is easy to understand why fruit plays such a central role in our diet.

When energy levels are low, a few grapes, a banana, apricots or an apple, whether fresh or dried, revitalize us in a few moments. Fruit provides the perfect guilt-free snack since most varieties are fat-free and contain very few calories. Nearly all fruits have a high proportion of water, which makes them satisfyingly thirst-quenching in hot weather, instead of a drink at any time.

Cooked fruit, on the other hand, can make a wonderfully warming and comforting pudding when the days are cold and dreary. No wonder we can't wait for winter to tuck into satisfying sweets like Blueberry and Pear Pie or favourites like Apple Pie.

Fruit is amazingly versatile. You could easily base an entire meal on it without repeating any colours, textures or flavours. Starting with Thai Chicken and Citrus Soup, you could progress to Venison with Cranberry Sauce, and finish with a flourish by serving Fresh Raspberry and Passion Fruit Chinchilla Soufflés. Fruit and cheese are classic companions, so you could as easily end with a platter of fine cheeses accompanied by grapes, pears and apples, or dried fruit and nuts.

Fruit is no longer the seasonal produce it once was. Nowadays, thanks to sophisticated transportation methods, all types of fruit from every country are available almost all year round. Travellers who have sampled exotic produce abroad now find it gracing the shelves of their local greengrocer or supermarket, giving them a taste of the tropical climates at home and a chance to experiment with new recipes.

There is nothing to beat the flavour of freshly picked fruit, however; sinking your teeth into a fresh strawberry, or taking a bite out of an apple that only seconds ago was on the tree, are two of life's greatest pleasures, only to be equalled by transforming such superb ingredients into delicious dishes.

PREPARING FRUIT

For some fruits, the only preparation needed is washing or wiping with a damp cloth; others must be peeled, skinned, cored, stoned or seeded. The skin protects and preserves fruit so wash and peel it just before using to conserve its freshness.

FIRM FRUIT

PEELING

Some firm fruits, such as dessert apples and pears, can be eaten raw without peeling. For cooking, peeling is often necessary. Pare off the skin as thinly as possible to avoid losing the valuable nutrients under the skin.

Wash the fruit and pat dry using kitchen paper. Use a small, sharp paring knife or a vegetable peeler to pare off the skin in long, thin vertical strips. Pears are best peeled by this method. For apples, thinly peel all round the fruit in a spiral.

CORING

To core whole apples and pears, place the sharp edge of a corer over the stem end of the fruit. Press down firmly, then twist slightly; the core, complete with pips, will come away in the centre of the corer. Push out the core from the handle end.

SEGMENTING

Halve the fruit lengthways, then cut into quarters or segments.

Carefully cut out the central core and pips, with a small sharp knife.

CITRUS FRUIT

PEELING

It is very important to remove all of the bitter white pith that lies just beneath the rind of citrus fruits.

To peel firm-skinned fruits, hold the fruit over a bowl to catch the juice and use a sharp knife to cut off the rind.

For loose-skinned fruit, such as tangerines, pierce the skin with your forefinger at the stalk end and peel off the rind. Pull off all the white shreds adhering to the fruit.

SEGMENTING

Use a small serrated knife to cut down in between the membranes enclosing the segments; cut along both sides and the base of the segment then carefully ease out the flesh of the fruit.

GRATING

Citrus zest adds a wonderful flavour to many dishes. If it is to be eaten raw, grate it finely, using the fine face of a grater. Remove only the coloured zest; if you grate too deeply into the peel, you will be in danger of including the bitter white pith. For cooking, pare off long, thin strips of zest using a zester. These thin strips also make a stylish garnish.

Make sure that you use a whole lemon that has good, firm flesh; soft loose skin will not grate easily. Hold the grater over a bowl, or stand on a board to collect the rind.

SOFT FRUIT

PEELING

Fruits, such as peaches, nectarines and apricots can be peeled with a sharp paring knife, but this may waste some of the delicious flesh. It is better to loosen the skins by dipping them briefly in boiling water.

Make a tiny nick in the skin. Cover with boiling water and leave for 15–30 seconds, depending on the ripeness of the fruit. Remove the fruit with ·a slotted spoon and peel off the skin, which should come away easily.

COOKING FRUIT

There are some fruits that many people wouldn't consider cooking, but most fruit can be cooked in a variety of ways. A few experiments can yield quite delicious results.

GRILLING

Any firm fruits can be grilled, with or without sugar. Tropical fruits, such as pineapple and bananas, are particularly good for grilling. For desserts, they can be cut into 2.5cm/1in wedges or chunks and threaded on to skewers to make kebabs. Brush the fruit with clear honey before grilling.

Halve the fruit or cut into pieces, removing the core if necessary. Brush with melted butter and grill under a medium heat, turning occasionally until tender and browned on all sides.

POACHING

Apples and pears, stone fruits, figs, rhubarb and even grapes can be poached, either whole, halved or in segments. The classic poaching liquid is syrup and usually consists of 1 part sugar boiled with 2 parts water for about 2 minutes or until clear. The syrup can be flavoured with lemon, orange or spices, such as cinnamon or vanilla. Red or white wine can also be used.

Bring the poaching liquid to the boil. Lower the heat and add the fruit. Simmer gently until the fruit is just tender.

BAKING

Apples and pears, stone fruits, such as peaches, nectarines, apricots and plums, as well as figs and rhubarb can be baked whole or in halves, wedges or slices according to type. If you want the fruit to remain very moist add a few drops of water to the cooking dish and cover with a lid.

Put the fruit in a shallow ovenproof dish, add a little water, and sprinkle with sugar to taste. Top the fruit with small pieces of butter. Bake in a preheated oven at 180°C/ 350°F/Gas 4 until tender.

DEEP FRYING

For fruit fritters, such as pineapple, apple or banana, peel the fruit and cut into chunks, thick slices or, if they are not too large, deep fry them whole.

Heat oil for deep frying to 185°C/360°F or until a cube of dried bread sizzles when it is added to the pan. Coat the pieces of fruit in batter and deep fry until the fritters rise to the surface of the hot oil and are golden brown. Drain the fritters on kitchen paper and sprinkle with sugar.

PUREEING

Fruit can be puréed for sauces, fools, sauces, ice creams and sorbets. Some types must be cooked first; others, like berries, can be puréed raw.

For cooked, peeled fruit, mash with a potato masher for a coarse purée. For a finer purée, whizz cooked, peeled fruit in a food processor or push through a food mill or sieve.

For berries, wash briefly and push through a fine nylon sieve, using the back of a large spoon or ladle. If you prefer, purée the berries in a food processor, then sieve the purée to remove any pips, small pieces of skin or stalks.

CARAMELIZING

Fruits glisten and look pretty when caramelized. Small fruits like blackcurrants, grapes, cherries and raspberries can be used whole. Larger fruits should be cubed.

Combine 200g/7oz/scant 1 cup granulated sugar and 60ml/4 tbsp water in a small heavy-based saucepan. Stir over a low heat until the sugar has dissolved. When the mixture boils, add 5ml/1 tsp lemon juice and boil until the syrup turns a deep golden brown.

Add 15ml/1 tbsp hot water and shake the pan to mix. Spear a piece of fruit on a fork and dip it into the caramel to coat. Leave on an oiled baking sheet until the caramel cools and hardens.

starters and side dishes

Many sweet and sharp-flavoured fruits can be combined

successfully with savoury ingredients to make wonderful

first-course dishes that stimulate the appetite for the

meal to come, and side dishes that are the perfect

complement to a main course. The following recipes

marry flavours to great effect, creating an intriguing

range of taste sensations.

THAI CHICKEN AND CITRUS SOUP

An exotic and aromatic soup that combines delicious flavours from South-East Asia.

Serves 4

15ml/1 tbsp vegetable oil

1 garlic clove, finely chopped

2 boned chicken breasts (about 175g/
   6oz each), skinned and chopped

2.5ml/½ tsp ground turmeric

1.5ml/¼ tsp hot chilli powder

75g/3oz creamed coconut

900ml/1½ pints/3¾ cups hot
   chicken stock

30ml/2 tbsp lemon juice

30ml/2 tbsp crunchy peanut butter

50g/2oz/1 cup thread egg noodles,
   broken into small pieces

15ml/1 tbsp chopped spring onions

15ml/1 tbsp chopped fresh coriander

salt and ground black pepper

30ml/2 tbsp desiccated coconut and ½
   fresh red chilli, seeded and finely
   chopped, to garnish

Heat the oil in a large pan and fry the garlic for 1 minute until lightly golden. Add the chicken, turmeric and chilli powder and stir-fry for a further 3–4 minutes.

Crumble the creamed coconut into the hot chicken stock and stir until dissolved. Pour on to the chicken and add the lemon juice, peanut butter and egg noodles. Stir well, to mix.

Cover the pan and simmer for about 15 minutes. Add the spring onions and fresh coriander, then season well and cook for a further 5 minutes.

Meanwhile, place the coconut and chilli in a small frying pan and heat for 2–3 minutes, stirring frequently, until the coconut is lightly browned.

Serve the soup in bowls sprinkled with the fried coconut and chilli.

PARSNIP AND APPLE SOUP

A hearty, warming soup that's excellent served on a cold winter's day.

Serves 8–10

50g/2oz/4 tbsp unsalted butter
2 large onions, sliced
1 garlic clove, chopped
2 large parsnips, scrubbed and cubed
2 cooking apples (about 450g/1lb),
  peeled, cored and cubed
10ml/2 tsp medium curry powder
1.5 litres/2½ pints/6¼ cups
  chicken stock
300ml/½ pint/1¼ cups single cream
salt and ground black pepper

For the topping
25g/1oz/2 tbsp unsalted butter
115g/4oz/1 cup pecans, chopped
150ml/¼ pint/⅔ cup crème fraîche or
  soured cream

Heat the butter in a large pan and sauté the onions and garlic over moderate heat until the onions are translucent. Stir in the parsnips and apples and sauté for a further 3 minutes, stirring occasionally. Add the curry powder and stir to mix. Cook for 1 minute more. Pour on the stock, bring to the boil, cover the pan and simmer for 20 minutes. Remove from the heat and cool slightly. Pour into a food processor or blender and process until smooth. Return the soup to the pan. Stir in the cream and seasoning and heat gently.

To make the topping, heat the butter in a pan and sauté the pecans over moderate heat for 5 minutes. Serve the soup in bowls topped with the crème fraîche or soured cream and sprinkled with the sautéed pecans.

FIG, APPLE AND DATE SALAD

Sweet Mediterranean figs and dates combine especially well with crisp eating apples.

Serves 4

6 large eating apples

juice of ¹/₂ lemon

175g/6oz fresh dates

25g/1oz white marzipan

5ml/1 tsp orange flower water

60ml/4 tbsp natural yogurt

4 fresh green or purple figs

4 toasted almonds, to garnish

COOK'S TIP

When buying fresh dates, avoid
any that look shrivelled. They
should be plump and shiny,
yellow-red to golden brown and
with smooth skins.

Core the apples and slice thinly with a sharp knife. Leave the skins on. Cut into fine matchsticks. Place in a bowl and moisten with lemon juice.

Remove the stones from the dates and cut the flesh into fine strips, then combine with the apple slices in the bowl.

In a separate bowl, soften the marzipan with orange flower water and combine with the yogurt. Mix together well until smooth.

Divide the apples and dates among the centre of four plates. Remove the stem from each of the figs and divide the fruit into quarters without cutting right through the base. Squeeze the base with the thumb and forefinger of each hand to open up the fruit. Place a fig in the centre of each salad, spoon in the yogurt filling and serve garnished with a toasted almond.

PLANTAIN AND GREEN BANANA SALAD

Cooking plantains and bananas in their skins helps to retain the soft texture so that they absorb all the flavour of the dressing.

Serves 4

2 ripe yellow plantains

3 green bananas

1 garlic clove, crushed

1 red onion

15–30ml/1–2 tbsp chopped
*   fresh coriander*

45ml/3 tbsp sunflower oil

25ml/1½ tbsp malt vinegar

salt and coarse-grain black pepper

Slit the plantains and bananas lengthways along their natural ridges, then cut in half and place in a large saucepan. Pour in water to cover, add a little salt and bring to the boil.

Boil the plantains and bananas gently for 20 minutes until tender, then drain well. When they are cool enough to handle, peel and cut them into medium-sized slices.

Put the plantain and banana slices into a bowl and add the crushed garlic, turning to mix.

Cut the onion in half and slice it thinly. Add to the bowl with the chopped fresh coriander, oil and vinegar. Add salt and pepper to taste. Toss to mix, then serve.

COOK'S TIP
Red onions are mild and sweet, so they are ideal for mixing in salads and for adding extra flavour to sandwiches.

FRESH BERRY SALSA

This bright, tangy salsa is spicy hot – add more chilli if you would like to make it even more fiery. It is good served with grilled chicken or fish.

Serves 4–6

1 fresh chilli

½ red onion, minced

2 spring onions, chopped

1 tomato, finely diced

1 small yellow pepper, seeded and finely chopped

10g/¼oz/¼ cup chopped fresh coriander

1.5ml/¼ tsp salt

15ml/1 tbsp raspberry vinegar

15ml/1 tbsp fresh orange juice

5ml/1 tsp honey

15ml/1 tbsp olive oil

150g/5oz/1 cup strawberries

115g/4oz/1 cup blueberries or blackberries

175g/6oz/1 cup raspberries

Finely chop the chilli (discard the seeds and membrane if a less hot flavour is desired) and place in a large bowl.

Add the red onion, spring onions, tomato, pepper, and coriander and stir together to blend well.

To make the dressing, whisk together the salt, vinegar, orange juice, honey and oil in a small bowl. Pour over the chilli mixture and stir well.

Hull the strawberries, rinse and pat dry if necessary. Coarsely chop the strawberries, then add to the chilli mixture with the blueberries or blackberries and raspberries, and stir to blend. Leave the mixture to stand at room temperature for 3 hours or until required.

Serve the salsa at room temperature.

SPINACH PLANTAIN ROUNDS

This delectable way of serving plantains is a little fiddly to make, but well worth the trouble. The plantains must be ripe, but still firm.

Serves 4

2 large yellow plantains, peeled
oil, for frying
30ml/2 tbsp butter
25g/1oz/1 tbsp finely chopped onion
2 garlic cloves, crushed
450g/1lb fresh spinach, chopped
pinch of freshly grated nutmeg
1 egg, beaten
wholemeal flour, for dusting
salt and ground black pepper

Using a small, sharp knife, carefully cut each plantain lengthways into four slices. Heat a little oil in a large frying pan and fry the slices on both sides until pale gold in colour, but not fully cooked. Lift out and drain on kitchen paper and reserve the oil in the frying pan.

Melt the butter in a saucepan and sauté the onion and garlic for 2–3 minutes until the onion is soft. Add the spinach and nutmeg, with salt and pepper to taste. Cover and cook for about 5 minutes until the spinach has reduced. Cool, then tip into a sieve, and press out any excess moisture.

Curl the plantain slices into rings and secure each ring with a wooden cocktail stick. Pack each ring with a little of the spinach mixture.

Place the egg and flour in two separate shallow dishes. Add a little more oil to the frying pan, if necessary, and heat until moderately hot. Dip the plantain rings in the egg and then in the flour and fry on both sides for 1–2 minutes until golden brown. Drain on kitchen paper and serve hot or cold.

COOK'S TIP

If fresh spinach is not available, use frozen spinach. Thaw completely and drain thoroughly in a sieve before cooking.

STEAMED BANANA LEAF PARCELS

Very neat and delicate, these steamed seafood packets from Thailand make an excellent starter or light lunch.

Serves 4

225g/8oz crab meat

50g/2oz peeled prawns, chopped

6 drained water chestnuts, chopped

30ml/2 tbsp chopped bamboo shoots

15ml/1 tbsp chopped spring onion

5ml/1 tsp chopped fresh root ginger

30ml/2 tbsp soy sauce

15ml/1 tbsp fish sauce

12 rice sheets

banana leaves, for lining steamer

oil for brushing

2 spring onions, shredded, 2 fresh red chillies, seeded and sliced, and coriander leaves, to garnish

COOK'S TIP

The seafood packets will spread out when cooked so be sure to space them well apart in the steamer to prevent them sticking together.

Combine the crab meat, chopped prawns, chestnuts, bamboo shoots, spring onion and ginger in a bowl. Mix well, then add 15ml/1 tbsp of the soy sauce and all the fish sauce. Stir until blended.

Take a rice sheet and dip it in warm water. Place it on a flat surface and leave for a few seconds to soften.

Place a spoonful of the filling in the centre of the sheet and fold into a square packet. Repeat with the rest of the rice sheets and seafood mixture.

Use banana leaves to line a steamer, then brush them with oil. Place the packets, seam side down, on the leaves and steam over a high heat for 6–8 minutes or until the filling is cooked. Transfer to a plate and garnish with the spring onions, chillies and coriander leaves.

ASPARAGUS WITH CREAMY RASPBERRY VINAIGRETTE

This simple starter is an unusual and delicious way to serve the first raspberries of the summer.

Serves 4

675g/1¹/₂lb thin asparagus spears
30ml/2 tbsp raspberry vinegar
2.5ml/¹/₂ tsp salt
5ml/1 tsp Dijon mustard
75ml/5 tbsp sunflower oil
30ml/2 tbsp soured cream or
   plain yogurt
white pepper
175g/6oz/1 cup fresh raspberries

Fill a large wide pan or wok with 10cm/4in water and bring to the boil. Trim the ends of the asparagus spears. If desired, remove the "scales" using a vegetable peeler. Tie the asparagus into two bundles. Lower the bundles into the boiling water and cook for 2 minutes, until just tender.

With a slotted spoon, carefully remove the asparagus bundles from the boiling water and immerse in cold water to stop the cooking. Drain and untie the bundles. Pat dry with kitchen paper. Chill the asparagus at least 1 hour.

Put the vinegar and salt in a bowl and stir with a fork until dissolved. Stir in the mustard, then gradually stir in the oil until blended. Add the soured cream or yogurt and pepper to taste.

To serve, place the asparagus on individual plates and drizzle the dressing across the middle of the spears. Garnish with the fresh raspberries.

savoury dishes

By partnering fruit with vegetables, fish, seafood,

poultry, game or meat, quite stunningly successful

savoury dishes, many of them with an international

flavour, can be created. Here you will find plenty of

inspiration for mouthwatering main meals, lunches, and

extra special recipes perfect for

entertaining.

LEMON AND GINGER SPICY BEANS

An extremely quick delicious meal, made with canned beans for speed.

Serves 4

30ml/2 tbsp chopped fresh root ginger

3 garlic cloves, roughly chopped

250ml/8fl oz/1 cup cold water

15ml/1 tbsp sunflower oil

1 large onion, thinly sliced

*1 fresh red chilli, seeded and finely
  chopped*

1.5ml/¼ tsp cayenne pepper

10ml/2 tsp ground cumin

5ml/1 tsp ground coriander

2.5ml/½ tsp ground turmeric

30ml/2 tbsp lemon juice

*15g/½oz/½ cup chopped fresh
  coriander*

*400g/14oz can black-eyed beans,
  drained and rinsed*

*400g/14oz can aduki beans, drained
  and rinsed*

*400g/14oz can haricot beans, drained
  and rinsed*

salt and ground black pepper

Place the ginger, garlic and 60ml/4 tbsp of the cold water in a blender or food processor and blend until smooth. Set aside.

Heat the oil in a pan. Add the onion and red chilli and cook gently for about 5 minutes until softened.

Add the cayenne pepper, cumin, ground coriander and turmeric and stir-fry for 1 minute.

Stir in the ginger and garlic paste from the blender and cook for another minute, stirring to prevent sticking.

Add the remaining water, lemon juice and fresh coriander, stir well and bring to the boil. Cover the pan tightly and cook for 5 minutes.

Add all the beans and cook for a further 5–10 minutes. Season with salt and pepper to taste and serve.

APPLE, ONION AND GRUYERE TART

Serve this tart with baked potatoes for a more filling meal.

Serves 4

1 large onion, finely chopped
25g/1oz/2 tbsp butter
1 large or 2 small eating apples,
  peeled and grated
2 size 1 eggs
150ml/¼ pint/⅔ cup double cream
1.5ml/¼ tsp dried mixed herbs
2.5ml/½ tsp dry mustard powder
115g/4oz Gruyère cheese
salt and ground black pepper
green salad leaves, to serve

For the pastry

225g/8oz/2 cups plain flour
1.5ml/¼ tsp dry mustard powder
75g/3oz/6 tbsp soft margarine
75g/3oz/6 tbsp Gruyère cheese,
  finely grated

COOK'S TIP
Instead of Gruyère, try Cheddar
or Lancashire cheese.

For the pastry, sift the flour, a pinch of salt and the mustard into a bowl. Rub in the margarine and cheese, add 30ml/2 tbsp water and form into a ball. Chill. Cook the onion in the butter for 10 minutes until softened. Stir in the apple and cook for 2–3 minutes. Leave to cool. Roll out the pastry and line a lightly greased 20cm/8in springform tin. Chill for 20 minutes. Preheat the oven to 200°C/400°F/Gas 6. Line the pastry with greaseproof paper and fill with baking beans. Bake for 20 minutes. Beat together the eggs, cream, herbs, seasoning and mustard. Grate three-quarters of the cheese and stir into this mixture. Slice the remaining cheese.

When the pastry is cooked, remove the paper and beans, add the onion mixture and pour in the egg mixture. Arrange the sliced cheese on top. Turn the oven down to 190°C/375°F/Gas 5. Bake for 20 minutes, until golden.

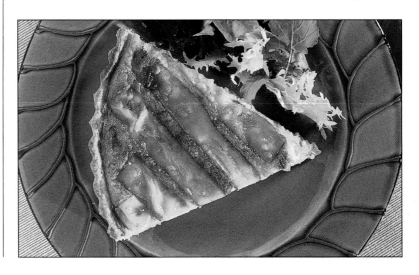

BANANA CURRY

The sweetness of the bananas combines well with the spices used to produce a mild, sweet curry.

Serves 4

4 under-ripe bananas

30ml/2 tbsp ground coriander

15ml/1 tbsp ground cumin

5ml/1 tsp chilli powder

2.5ml/½ tsp salt

1.5ml/¼ tsp ground turmeric

5ml/1 tsp granulated sugar

15ml/1 tbsp gram flour

45ml/3 tbsp chopped fresh coriander

90ml/6 tbsp corn oil

1.5ml/¼ tsp cumin seeds

1.5ml/¼ tsp black mustard seeds

fresh coriander sprigs, to garnish

chappatis, to serve

COOK'S TIP
Choose bananas that are slightly under-ripe so that they retain their shape and do not become unpleasantly mushy when they are cooked.

Trim the bananas, leaving the skin on, and cut each into three equal pieces. Make a lengthways slit in each piece of banana, without cutting through.

Mix the ground coriander, cumin, chilli powder, salt, turmeric, sugar, gram flour and chopped coriander in a soup plate. Stir in 15ml/1 tbsp of the oil. Carefully stuff each piece of banana with the spice mixture, taking care not to break them in half.

Heat the remaining oil in a large heavy-based saucepan and fry the cumin and mustard seeds for 2 minutes or until they begin to splutter. Add the bananas and toss gently in the oil. Cover and simmer over a low heat for 15 minutes, stirring from time to time, until the bananas are soft, but not mushy. Garnish with the fresh coriander and serve with warm chappatis.

PLANTAIN AND VEGETABLE KEBABS

Tasty and colourful, these kebabs make a delightful main course for vegetarians or can be served as a side dish.

Serves 4

115g/4oz pumpkin, peeled and cubed

1 red onion, cut into wedges

1 small courgette, sliced

1 yellow plantain, sliced

1 aubergine, diced

½ red pepper, seeded and diced

½ green pepper, seeded and diced

12 button mushrooms, trimmed

60ml/4 tbsp lemon juice

60ml/4 tbsp olive or sunflower oil

45–60ml/3–4 tbsp soy sauce

150ml/¼ pint/⅔ cup tomato juice

*1 fresh green chilli, seeded
    and chopped*

½ onion, grated

3 garlic cloves, crushed

*7.5ml/1½ tsp dried
    tarragon, crushed*

*4ml/¾ tsp each dried basil, dried
    thyme and ground cinnamon*

25g/1oz/2 tbsp butter

300ml/½ pint/1¼ cups vegetable stock

freshly ground black pepper

Place the pumpkin in a small bowl and cover with boiling water. Blanch for 2–3 minutes, then drain, refresh under cold water, drain again and tip into a large bowl. Add the red onion, courgette, plantain, aubergine, peppers and mushrooms.

Mix the lemon juice, oil, soy sauce, tomato juice, chilli, grated onion, garlic, herbs, cinnamon and black pepper in a jug. Pour over the vegetables. Toss well, then set aside in a cool place to marinate for 3–4 hours.

Drain the vegetables and thread them alternately on to eight skewers. Grill under a low heat for about 15 minutes, turning the kebabs frequently, until golden brown. Baste occasionally with the marinade to keep the vegetables moist.

Place the remaining marinade, butter and stock in a pan and bring to the boil. Lower the heat and simmer for 10 minutes to cook the onion and reduce the sauce. Pour into a serving jug. Arrange the vegetable skewers on a plate. Serve with a rice dish or salad.

SEAFOOD KEBABS WITH GINGER AND LIME

This fragrant marinade will guarantee a mouth-watering aroma from the barbecue, and it is equally delicious with chicken or pork.

Serves 4–6

*500g/1¼lb prawns and cubed
  monkfish*
*selection of prepared vegetables, such
  as red, green or orange peppers,
  courgettes, button mushrooms, red
  onion, bay leaves, cherry tomatoes*

For the marinade
3 limes
15ml/1 tbsp green cardamom pods
1 onion, finely chopped
15ml/1 tbsp grated fresh root ginger
*1 large garlic clove, skinned
  and crushed*
45ml/3 tbsp olive oil

First make the marinade. Finely grate the rind from one lime and squeeze the juice from all of them. Split the cardamom pods and remove the seeds.  Crush the cardamom seeds in a pestle and mortar or with the back of a heavy-bladed knife.

Place the lime rind and juice, crushed cardamom, onion, root ginger, garlic and olive oil in a small bowl and mix together thoroughly. Pour the marinade over the prawns and monkfish, stir gently, then cover and leave in a cool place for 2–3 hours.

Thread four skewers alternately with the prawns, monkfish, vegetables and bay leaves. Cook slowly under a hot grill or over a barbecue, basting occasionally with the marinade, until the prawns, fish and vegetables are just cooked through and browned on the outside. Serve at once.

CLASSIC FISH PIE WITH LEMON

Instead of a potato topping, a crust of puff pastry could be used for a change.

Serves 4

*450g/1lb mixed raw fish such
   as cod or salmon fillets and
   peeled prawns*
finely grated rind of 1 lemon
450g/1lb floury potatoes
40g/1½ oz flour/3 tbsp butter
150ml/¼ pint/⅔ cup milk
*45ml/3 tbsp chopped fresh parsley,
   plus extra to garnish*
1 egg
salt and ground black pepper

Preheat the oven to 220°C/425°F/Gas 7. Grease a 600ml/1 pint/2 cup ovenproof dish. Cut the fish into bite-sized pieces. Season the fish, sprinkle over the lemon rind and place in the base of the dish. Cook the potatoes in boiling, salted water until tender.

Meanwhile, make the sauce. Melt a third of the butter in a saucepan, add the flour and cook for a few minutes. Remove from the heat and gradually whisk in the milk. Return to the heat and bring to the boil. Simmer, whisking all the time, until the sauce has thickened. Add the parsley and season to taste. Pour over the fish.

Drain and mash the potatoes, adding the remaining butter. Pipe or spoon the potatoes on top of the fish mixture. Beat the egg and brush over the potato. Bake in the oven for 45 minutes until the top is golden. Serve, garnished with parsley.

GRILLED SNAPPER WITH MANGO SALSA

A ripe mango is used in this fruity salsa with the tropical flavours of coriander, ginger and chilli.

Serves 4

350g/12oz new potatoes

3 eggs

115g/4oz French beans, topped, tailed and halved

4 × 350g/12oz red snapper, scaled and gutted

30ml/2 tbsp olive oil

175g/6oz mixed lettuce leaves, such as frisée or Webb's

2 cherry tomatoes

salt and ground black pepper

For the salsa

45ml/3 tbsp chopped fresh coriander

1 medium-size ripe mango, peeled, stoned and diced

1/2 red chilli, seeded and chopped

15ml/1 tbsp grated fresh root ginger

juice of 2 limes

generous pinch of celery salt

Bring the potatoes to the boil and simmer for 15–20 minutes. Drain. Bring a second large saucepan of salted water to the boil. Put in the eggs and boil for 4 minutes, then add the beans and cook for a further 6 minutes. Remove the eggs from the pan, cool, peel and cut into quarters. Preheat a moderate grill. Slash the snappers on each side, moisten with oil and cook for 12 minutes, turning once. To make the salsa, place the coriander in a blender or food processor. Add the remaining ingredients and process until smooth.

Arrange the lettuce on four large plates. Arrange the snapper over the lettuce and season to taste. Halve the potatoes and tomatoes, and add with the beans and eggs to the salad. Serve with the salsa.

FISH WITH MANGO AND GINGER DRESSING

The tasty dressing for this salad combines the flavour of rich mango with ginger, hot chilli and lime.

Serves 4

1 French loaf

4 red mullet or snapper, each weighing
about 275g/10oz

15ml/1 tbsp vegetable oil

1 mango

15ml/1 tbsp grated fresh root ginger

1 fresh red chilli, seeded and
finely chopped

30ml/2 tbsp lime juice

30ml/2 tbsp chopped fresh coriander

175g/6oz young spinach

175g/6oz cherry tomatoes, halved,
to garnish

COOK'S TIP

Other varieties of fish that are
suitable for this salad include
salmon, monkfish, tuna, sea
bass and halibut.

Preheat the oven to 180°C/350°F/Gas 4. Cut the French loaf into 20cm/8in lengths. Slice lengthways, then cut into thick fingers. Place the bread on a baking sheet and dry in the oven for 15 minutes. Preheat the grill. Slash the fish on both sides and moisten with oil. Grill for about 6 minutes, turning once. Slice one half of the mango and reserve. Place the remainder in a blender or food processor. Add the ginger, chilli, lime juice and coriander. Process until smooth. Adjust to a pouring consistency with 30–45ml/2–3 tbsp water. Wash and dry the spinach, then arrange on four plates. Place the fish over the leaves. Spoon on the mango dressing and serve with mango slices, tomato halves, and the French bread.

GRILLED FRESH SARDINES

*Fresh sardines are flavourful and firm-fleshed, and quite different in taste and consistency from those
canned in oil. They are excellent simply grilled and served with lemon.*

Serves 4–6

*1kg/2lb very fresh sardines, gutted and
  with heads removed*
olive oil, for brushing
salt and ground black pepper
*45ml/3 tbsp chopped fresh parsley,
  to serve*
lemon wedges, to garnish

Preheat the grill. Rinse the sardines in water. Pat dry with kitchen paper.
Brush the sardines lightly with olive oil and sprinkle generously with salt
and ground black pepper. Place the sardines in one layer on the grill pan.
Grill the sardines for about 3–4 minutes.

Turn the sardines over, and cook for 3–4 minutes more, or until the skin
begins to brown. Serve immediately, sprinkled with parsley and garnished
with lemon wedges.

WHITING FILLETS IN A LEMONY POLENTA CRUST

Polenta is the name given to fine golden cornmeal. Use the quick and easy polenta if you can as it will give a better crunchy coating for the fish.

Serves 4

8 small whiting fillets
finely grated rind of 2 lemons
225g/8oz/2 cups polenta
30ml/2 tbsp olive oil
15ml/1 tbsp butter
salt and ground black pepper
steamed spinach, to serve
toasted pine nuts, ¹/₂ red onion, finely
  sliced, and 30ml/2 tbsp mixed fresh
  herbs such as parsley, chervil and
  chives, to garnish

Make four small cuts in each whiting fillet, with a sharp knife, to prevent the fish curling up when it is cooked.

Sprinkle the seasoning and half of the lemon rind over the fish.

Mix the polenta with the remaining lemon rind. Press the polenta on to the fillets. Chill for 30 minutes.

Heat the oil and butter in a large frying pan and gently fry the fillets on either side for 3–4 minutes. Serve with steamed spinach and garnish with toasted pine nuts, red onion slices and the mixed fresh herbs.

SALMON WITH LEMON AND HERB BUTTER

Cooking "en papillote" preserves and enhances the flavour of salmon in this simple but delectable recipe.

Serves 4

50g/2oz/4 tbsp butter, softened
finely grated rind of ½ small lemon
15ml/1 tbsp lemon juice
15ml/1 tbsp chopped fresh dill
4 salmon steaks, about 150g/5oz each
2 lemon slices, halved
4 fresh dill sprigs
salt and ground black pepper

Place the butter, lemon rind, lemon juice, chopped dill and seasoning in a small bowl and mix together with a fork until blended.

Spoon the butter on to a piece of greaseproof paper and roll up, smoothing with your hands into a sausage shape. Twist the ends tightly, wrap in clear film and pop in the freezer for 20 minutes, until firm.

Meanwhile, preheat the oven to 190°C/375°F/Gas 5. Cut out four squares of foil big enough to encase the salmon steaks and grease lightly. Place a salmon steak in the centre of each one.

Remove the butter from the freezer and slice into eight rounds. Place two rounds on top of each salmon steak with a halved lemon slice in the centre and a sprig of dill on top. Lift up the edges of the foil and crinkle them together until well sealed.

Lift the parcels on to a baking sheet and bake for about 20 minutes. Remove from the oven and place the unopened parcels on warmed plates. Open the parcels and slide the contents on to the plates with the juices.

COOK'S TIP

A different selection of fresh herbs could be used to flavour the butter – try mint, fennel fronds, lemon balm, parsley or oregano instead of the dill.

SEA BASS WITH CITRUS FRUIT

Along the Mediterranean coast, sea bass is called loup de mer; *elsewhere in France it is known as* bar. *Its delicate flavour is complemented by citrus fruits and fruity French olive oil.*

Serves 6

1 lemon

1 orange

1 small grapefruit

1 sea bass (about 1.35kg/3lb), cleaned and scaled

6 fresh basil sprigs

6 fresh dill sprigs

plain flour, for dusting

45ml/3 tbsp French olive oil

4–6 shallots, peeled and halved

60ml/4 tbsp dry white wine

15g/¹/₂oz/1 tbsp butter

salt and ground black pepper

fresh dill, to garnish

With a vegetable peeler, remove the rind from the lemon, orange and grapefruit. Cut into thin julienne strips, cover and set aside. Peel off the white pith from the fruits and, working over a bowl to catch the juices, cut out the segments from the grapefruit and orange and set aside for the garnish. Slice the lemon thickly.

Preheat the oven to 190°C/375°F/Gas 5. Wipe the fish dry inside and out and season the cavity with salt and ground black pepper. Make three diagonal slashes on each side of the fish. Reserve a few basil and dill sprigs for the garnish and fill the cavity with the remaining basil and dill, the lemon slices and half the julienne strips of citrus rind.

Dust the fish lightly with flour. In a roasting tin or flameproof casserole large enough to hold the fish, heat 30ml/2 tbsp of the olive oil over a medium-high heat and cook the fish for about 1 minute until the skin just crisps and browns on one side. Add the shallots.

Place the fish in the oven and bake for about 15 minutes, then carefully turn the fish over and stir the shallots. Drizzle the fish with the remaining oil and bake for a further 10–15 minutes until the flesh is opaque throughout.

Carefully transfer the fish to a heated serving dish and remove and discard the cavity stuffing. Pour off any excess oil and add the wine and 30–45ml/2–3 tbsp of the fruit juices to the pan. Bring to the boil over a high heat, stirring. Stir in the remaining julienne strips of citrus rind and boil for 2–3 minutes, then whisk in the butter.

Spoon the shallots and sauce over the fish. Garnish with the reserved basil and dill, and the reserved grapefruit and orange segments.

BAKED FISH IN BANANA LEAVES

Fish baked in banana leaves is particularly succulent and flavourful. This is a great dish for barbecuing.

Serves 4

250ml/8 fl oz/1 cup coconut milk
30ml/2 tbsp red curry paste
45ml/3 tbsp fish sauce
30ml/2 tbsp caster sugar
5 kaffir lime leaves, torn
4 fish fillets, about 175g/6oz each
175g/6oz mixed vegetables, such as
 carrots or leeks, finely shredded
4 banana leaves

For the garnish

30ml/2 tbsp shredded spring onions
2 fresh red chillies, finely sliced

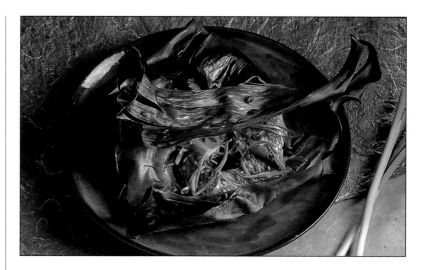

Combine the coconut milk, curry paste, fish sauce, sugar and kaffir lime leaves in a shallow dish. Add the fish and marinate for 15–30 minutes. Preheat the oven to 200°C/ 400°F/Gas 6.

Mix the selected vegetables together and place a quarter of the mixture on top of a banana leaf. Place a fish fillet on top of each and moisten it with a little of the marinade.

Wrap the fish up by turning in the sides and ends of the leaf and securing the package with cocktail sticks. Repeat with the rest of the leaves, vegetables and fish.

Bake for 20–25 minutes or until the fish is cooked. Alternatively, cook under the grill or in a hinged grill over a barbecue. Just before serving, garnish the fish with a sprinkling of spring onions and sliced red chillies.

CHICKEN STEW WITH BLACKBERRIES AND LEMON BALM

The combination of red wine and blackberries in this delicious stew gives it a dramatic appearance.

Serves 4

4 chicken breasts, partly boned

25g/1oz/2 tbsp butter

15ml/1 tbsp sunflower oil

25g/1oz/4 tbsp flour

150ml/¼ pint/⅔ cup red wine

150ml/¼ pint/⅔ cup chicken stock

grated rind of ½ orange plus
   15ml/1 tbsp juice

2 lemon balm sprigs, finely chopped,
   plus a few extra sprigs to garnish

150ml/¼ pint/⅔ cup double cream

1 egg yolk

salt and ground black pepper

100g/4oz/⅔ cup fresh blackberries,
   plus 50g/2oz/⅓ cup to garnish

Remove any skin from the chicken, and season the meat. Heat the butter and oil in a pan, fry the chicken to seal it, then transfer to a casserole. Stir the flour into the pan, then add wine and stock and bring to the boil. Add the orange rind and juice, and the lemon balm. Pour over the chicken.

Preheat the oven to 180°C/350°F/Gas 4. Cover the casserole and cook in the oven for about 40 minutes.

Blend the cream with the egg yolk, add some of the liquid from the casserole and stir back into the dish with the blackberries. Cover and cook for a further 10–15 minutes. Serve garnished with the rest of the blackberries and lemon balm sprigs.

TAGINE OF CHICKEN

Lemon slices add a decorative and tangy touch to this richly spiced North African dish.

Serves 8

8 chicken legs (thighs and drumsticks)
30ml/2 tbsp olive oil
1 medium onion, finely chopped
2 garlic cloves, crushed
5ml/1 tsp ground turmeric
2.5ml/¹/₂ tsp ground ginger
2.5ml/¹/₂ tsp ground cinnamon
450ml/³/₄ pint/1⁷/₈ cups chicken stock
150g/5oz/1¹/₄ cups green olives, stoned
1 lemon, sliced
salt and ground black pepper
fresh coriander sprigs, to garnish

For the vegetable couscous
600ml/1 pint/2¹/₂ cups chicken stock
450g/1lb couscous
4 courgettes, thickly sliced
2 carrots, thickly sliced
2 small turnips, peeled and cubed
45ml/3 tbsp olive oil
450g/15oz can chick-peas, drained
15ml/1 tbsp chopped fresh coriander

Preheat the oven to 180°C/350°F/Gas 4. Cut the chicken legs into two through the joint.

Heat the oil in a large flameproof casserole and, working in batches, brown the chicken on both sides. Remove and keep warm.

Add the onion and crushed garlic to the flameproof casserole and cook gently until tender. Add the spices and cook for 1 minute. Pour over the stock, bring to the boil, and return the chicken to the casserole. Cover and bake for 45 minutes until tender.

Transfer the chicken to a bowl, cover and keep warm. Remove any fat from the cooking liquid and boil to reduce by one third. Meanwhile, blanch the olives and lemon slices in a pan of boiling water for 2 minutes until the lemon skin is tender. Drain and add to the chicken with the reduced cooking liquid, adjusting the seasoning to taste.

To cook the couscous, bring the stock to the boil in a large pan and sprinkle in the couscous slowly, stirring all the time. Remove from the heat, cover and leave to stand for 5 minutes.

Meanwhile, cook the vegetables, drain and put them into a large bowl. Add the couscous and oil and season. Stir the grains to fluff them up, add the chick-peas and finally the chopped coriander. Spoon on to a large serving plate, cover with the chicken pieces, and spoon over the liquid. Garnish with fresh coriander sprigs.

HONEY AND ORANGE-GLAZED CHICKEN

Try orange-blossom honey for this tasty glaze. It makes a perfect partner for chicken and oranges.

Serve 4

*4 chicken breasts, about 175g/6oz
    each, boned and skinned*
15ml/1 tbsp oil
4 spring onions, chopped
1 garlic clove, crushed
45ml/3 tbsp clear honey
60ml/4 tbsp fresh orange juice
1 orange, peeled and segmented
30ml/2 tbsp soy sauce
*fresh lemon balm or flat leaf parsley
    sprigs, to garnish*
baked potatoes and salad, to serve

VARIATION

*The sauce is equally good when
served with pork steaks.*

Preheat the oven to 190°C/375°F/Gas 5. Place the chicken breasts in a shallow roasting tin and set aside.

Heat the oil in a small pan. Fry the spring onions and crushed garlic for 2 minutes until softened. Add the honey, orange juice, orange segments and soy sauce to the pan, stirring well until the honey has dissolved.

Pour the mixture over the chicken and bake, uncovered, for 45 minutes, basting once or twice, until the chicken is cooked through. Serve on plates, garnished with lemon balm or parsley, accompanied by baked potatoes and a fresh salad.

LEMON CHICKEN STIR-FRY

It is essential to prepare all the ingredients before you begin as this dish is cooked in minutes.

Serves 4

*4 chicken breasts (about 150g/5oz
  each), boned and skinned*

15ml/1 tbsp light soy sauce

75ml/5 tbsp cornflour

1 lemon

1 garlic clove, crushed

15ml/1 tbsp caster sugar

30ml/2 tbsp dry sherry

150ml/¼ pint/⅔ cup chicken stock

*juice and finely shredded rind of 1
  lemon*

60ml/4 tbsp olive oil

*1 bunch spring onions, sliced
  diagonally into 1cm/½in pieces*

salt and ground black pepper

Divide each chicken breast into two natural fillets. Place them between two sheets of clear film and flatten to a thickness of 5mm/¼in with a rolling pin. Cut into 2.5cm/1in strips across the fillets. Put the chicken into a bowl with the soy sauce and toss to coat. Toss in 60ml/4 tbsp cornflour.

Have ready the garlic clove, sugar, sherry, stock, lemon juice, lemon rind, and the remaining cornflour blended to a paste with cold water.

Heat the oil in a wok or large frying pan and cook the chicken in batches for 3–4 minutes. Remove and keep warm while frying the rest of the chicken.

Add the spring onions and garlic to the pan and cook for about 2 minutes. Add the remaining ingredients with the chicken and bring to the boil, stirring until thickened and the chicken is evenly covered with sauce. Serve immediately.

TURKEY BREASTS WITH LEMON AND SAGE

Lemon and sage combine to give a lively Mediterranean flavour to this dish.

Serves 4

*4 turkey cutlets (boneless slices of
   breast), about 175g/6oz each*
15ml/1 tbsp grated lemon rind
*15ml/1 tbsp chopped fresh sage, or
   5ml/1 tsp dried sage*
50ml/2fl oz/¼ cup fresh lemon juice
90ml/6 tbsp vegetable oil
115g/4oz/1 cup fine dry breadcrumbs
salt and ground black pepper
*fresh sage leaves and lemon slices,
   to garnish*

Place each cutlet between two sheets of greaseproof paper. With the flat side of a meat mallet, beat until about 5mm/¼in thick, being careful not to split the meat. Remove the greaseproof paper. Sprinkle the cutlets with salt and pepper.

In a small bowl, combine the lemon rind, chopped sage, lemon juice and 30ml/2 tbsp of the oil. Stir well to mix.

Arrange the turkey cutlets, in one layer, in one or two shallow baking dishes. Divide the lemon mixture evenly between the dishes and rub well into the turkey. Leave to marinate for 20 minutes.

Heat the remaining oil in a frying pan. Dredge the turkey breasts in the breadcrumbs, shaking off the excess. Fry until golden brown, about 2 minutes on each side. Serve the turkey breasts immediately, garnished with sage leaves and lemon slices.

VARIATION
*For a delicious alternative,
substitute fresh tarragon leaves
for the sage.*

GUINEA FOWL WITH CIDER AND APPLES

Guinea fowl are farmed, so they are available quite frequently in supermarkets, usually fresh. Their flavour is reminiscent of an old-fashioned chicken – not really gamey, but they do have slightly darker meat.

Serves 4

1.75kg/4–4½lb guinea fowl

1 onion, halved

3 celery sticks

3 bay leaves

a little butter

300ml/½ pint/1¼ cups dry cider

150ml/¼ pint/⅔ cup chicken stock

2 small cooking apples (about 450g/
  1lb), peeled and sliced

60ml/4 tbsp thick double cream

a few sage leaves, plus extra to garnish

30ml/2 tbsp chopped fresh parsley

salt and ground black pepper

If the guinea fowl is packed with its giblets, put them in a pan with water to cover, add half the onion, a stick of celery, a bay leaf and seasoning. Bring to the boil and simmer for about 30 minutes, or until you have about 150ml/¼ pint/⅔ cup of well-flavoured stock. Use this in the recipe instead of the chicken stock.

Preheat the oven to 190°C/375°F/Gas 5. Wash and wipe dry the bird and place the remaining onion half and a knob of butter inside the body cavity. Place the guinea fowl in a roasting dish, sprinkle with seasoning and dot with a few knobs of butter.

Pour the cider and chicken or home-made stock into the dish and cover with a lid or foil. Bake in the oven for 25 minutes per 450g/1lb, basting the bird occasionally.

Uncover for the last 20 minutes and baste well again. Slice the remaining celery and add it together with the prepared apples. When the guinea fowl is cooked, transfer it to a warm serving dish and keep warm. Remove the apples and celery with a slotted spoon and set aside.

Boil the liquid rapidly to reduce to about 150ml/¼ pint/⅔ cup. Stir in the cream, seasoning and the sage leaves, and cook for a few minutes more to reduce slightly. Return the apples to this pan with the parsley and warm through. Serve with or around the bird, garnished with sage leaves.

NORMANDY PHEASANT

Cider, apples and cream make this a rich, flavoursome dish – a great change from a plain roast.

Serves 4

2 oven-ready pheasants

15ml/1 tbsp olive oil

25g/1oz/2 tbsp butter

60ml/4 tbsp Calvados

450ml/³⁄4 pint/1⅞ cups dry cider

bouquet garni

3 Cox's Pippin, peeled, cored and
  thickly sliced

150ml/¼ pint/²⁄3 cup double cream

salt and ground black pepper

thyme sprigs, to garnish

Preheat the oven to 160°C/325°F/Gas 3. Joint both pheasants into four pieces using a large sharp knife. Discard the backbones and knuckles.

Heat the oil and butter in a large flameproof casserole. Working in two batches, add the pheasant pieces to the casserole and brown them over a high heat. Return all the pheasant pieces to the casserole.

Standing well back, pour over the Calvados and set it alight. When the flames have subsided, pour in the cider, then add the bouquet garni and seasoning and bring to the boil. Cover the casserole and cook in the oven for 50 minutes.

Tuck the apple slices around the pheasant. Cover and cook for about 5–10 minutes, or until the pheasant is tender. Transfer the pheasant and apple to a warmed serving plate. Keep warm.

Remove the bouquet garni, then boil the liquid to reduce the sauce by half until you have a syrupy consistency. Stir in the cream and simmer for a further 2–3 minutes until thickened. Taste the sauce and adjust the seasoning if necessary. Spoon the sauce over the pheasant and serve immediately garnished with thyme sprigs.

STIR-FRIED DUCK WITH BLUEBERRIES

Serve this conveniently quick dinner party dish with fresh mint sprigs, which will give a wonderful fresh
aroma as you bring the meal to the table.

Serves 4

2 duck breasts, about 175g/6oz each
30ml/2 tbsp sunflower oil
15ml/1 tbsp red wine vinegar
5ml/1 tsp sugar
5ml/1 tsp red wine
5ml/1 tsp crème de cassis
115g/4oz/1 cup fresh blueberries
15ml/1 tbsp chopped fresh mint
salt and ground black pepper
fresh mint sprigs, to garnish

Cut the duck breasts crossways into thin slices. Season well with salt and ground black pepper.

Heat a wok or large frying pan and add the oil. When the oil is hot, stir-fry the duck for 3 minutes.

Add the red wine vinegar, sugar, red wine and crème de cassis. Bubble for 3 minutes, to reduce to a thick syrup.

Stir in the blueberries, sprinkle over the chopped mint and then serve garnished with fresh mint sprigs.

LAMB, LEEK AND APPLE PIE

An innovative combination where lamb and leeks are spiced up with apple.

Serves 4

675g/1½lb lamb neck fillets, cut into
* 12 pieces*
115g/4oz gammon, diced
1 onion, thinly sliced
350g/12oz leeks, sliced
1 large cooking apple (about 225g/
* 8oz), peeled, cored and sliced*
1.5–2.5ml/¼–½ tsp ground allspice
1.5–2.5ml/¼–½ tsp grated nutmeg
150ml/¼ pint/⅔ cup lamb, beef or
* vegetable stock*
225g/8oz ready-made shortcrust pastry
beaten egg or milk, to glaze
salt and ground black pepper

COOK'S TIP
When you are buying leeks, look
for those that are straight and
well-shaped. Avoid any that
have yellow, discoloured and
slimy leaves.

Preheat the oven to 200°C/400°F/Gas 6. Layer the meats, onion, leeks and apple in a 900ml/1½ pint/3¾ cup pie dish, sprinkling in the spices and seasoning as you go. Pour in the stock.

On a lightly floured surface, roll out the pastry 2cm/¾in larger than the top of the pie dish. Cut a narrow strip from around the pastry, fit it around the dampened rim of the dish, then brush with water.

Lay the pastry over the filling and press the edges together to seal them. Brush the top with beaten egg or milk, and make a hole in the centre.

Bake the pie for 20 minutes, then reduce the oven temperature to 180°C/350°F/Gas 4 and continue to bake for 1–1¼ hours, covering the pie with foil if the pastry begins to become too brown. Serve immediately.

VENISON WITH CRANBERRY SAUCE

Venison steaks are now readily available. Lean and low in fat, they are the healthy choice for a special occasion. Served with a sauce of fresh seasonal cranberries, port and ginger, they make a delicious dish with a wonderful combination of flavours.

Serves 4

1 orange

1 lemon

*75g/3oz/³/₄ cup fresh or frozen
    cranberries*

5ml/1 tsp grated fresh root ginger

1 thyme sprig

5ml/1 tsp Dijon mustard

60ml/4 tbsp redcurrant jelly

150ml/¹/₄ pint/²/₃ cup ruby port

30ml/2 tbsp sunflower oil

4 venison steaks

2 shallots, finely chopped

salt and ground black pepper

thyme sprigs, to garnish

*creamy mashed potatoes and broccoli,
    to serve*

Pare the rind from half the orange and half the lemon using a vegetable peeler, then cut into very fine strips.

Blanch the strips in a small pan of boiling water for about 5 minutes until tender. Drain the strips and refresh under cold water.

Squeeze the juice from the orange and lemon and then pour into a small pan. Add the fresh or frozen cranberries, ginger, thyme sprig, mustard, redcurrant jelly and port. Cook over a low heat until the jelly melts.

Bring the sauce to the boil, stirring occasionally, then cover the pan and reduce the heat. Continue to cook gently, for about 15 minutes, until the cranberries are just tender.

Heat the oil in a heavy-based frying pan, add the venison steaks and cook over a high heat for 2–3 minutes.

Turn over the steaks and add the shallots to the pan. Cook the steaks on the other side for 2–3 minutes, depending on whether you like rare or medium-cooked meat.

Just before the end of cooking, pour in the sauce and add the strips of orange and lemon rind to the pan. Leave the sauce to bubble for a few seconds to thicken slightly, then remove the thyme sprig and adjust the seasoning to taste.

Transfer the venison steaks to warmed plates and spoon over the sauce. Garnish with thyme sprigs and serve accompanied by creamy mashed potatoes and broccoli.

BEEF STRIPS WITH ORANGE AND GINGER

Tender strips of beef, tangy ginger and crisp carrot make a simple but delicious stir-fry.

Serves 4

450g/1lb lean beef rump, fillet or
*   sirloin, cut into thin strips*
finely grated rind and juice of 1 orange
15ml/1 tbsp light soy sauce
5ml/1 tsp cornflour
15ml/1 tbsp finely chopped root ginger
10ml/2 tsp sesame oil
1 large carrot, cut into thin strips
2 spring onions, thinly sliced

Place the beef strips in a bowl and sprinkle over the orange rind and juice. Leave to marinate for at least 30 minutes.

Drain the liquid from the meat and set aside, then mix the meat with the soy sauce, cornflour and ginger until well combined.

Heat the oil in a wok or large frying pan and add the beef. Stir-fry for 1 minute until lightly coloured, then add the carrot and continue to stir-fry for a further 2–3 minutes.

Stir in the spring onions and reserved liquid, then cook, stirring, until boiling and thickened. Serve hot with rice noodles or plain boiled rice.

COOK'S TIP
Large wok lids are cumbersome
and can be difficult to store in a
small kitchen. Instead of using a
lid, place a circle of greaseproof
paper over the food surface to
retain the cooking juices.

PORK AND APPLE HOT-POT

An economical and tasty dish using a cheaper cut of pork.

Serves 4

500g/1¼lb sparerib pork chops

30ml/2 tbsp sunflower oil

1 large onion, sliced

3 celery sticks, chopped

15ml/1 tbsp chopped fresh sage, or
*   5ml/1 tsp dried*

15ml/1 tbsp chopped fresh parsley

2 eating apples, peeled, cored and cut
*   into thick wedges*

150ml/¼ pint/²⁄₃ cup apple juice

150ml/¼ pint/²⁄₃ cup lamb, beef or
*   vegetable stock*

15ml/1 tbsp cornflour

450g/1lb par-boiled, peeled and
*   sliced potatoes*

melted butter, to glaze

salt and ground black pepper

sage leaves, to garnish

Remove any bones from the pork and cut the meat into even-size cubes. Sprinkle with seasoning.

Heat the oil in a pan and fry the onion and celery until golden. Remove and place half in the base of a casserole. Arrange the meat on top and sprinkle with half the herbs.

Add the apples and the rest of the onion, celery and herbs. Season to taste. Blend the apple juice with the stock and cornflour and pour over.

Preheat the oven to 190°C/375°F/Gas 5. Top with the sliced potatoes and brush with melted butter. Cover and cook in the oven for 50–60 minutes, removing the lid for the last 15 minutes to brown the potatoes. Serve immediately, garnished with sage leaves.

SOMERSET PORK WITH APPLES

A rich country dish using fresh apples and cider.

Serves 4

25g/1oz/2 tbsp butter

500g/1¼lb pork loin, cut into bite-size
  pieces

12 baby onions, peeled

10ml/2 tsp grated lemon rind

300ml/½ pint/1¼ cups dry cider

150ml/¼ pint/⅔ cup veal stock

2 eating apples, cored and sliced

45ml/3 tbsp chopped fresh parsley

100ml/3½fl oz/scant ½ cup
  whipping cream

salt and ground black pepper

COOK'S TIP

It is advisable to remove the rind from the pork before cutting into pieces. This is best done with sharp scissors or a sharp knife.

Heat the butter in a large heavy-based frying pan and sauté the pork in batches until brown. Transfer the pork to a bowl.

Add the onions to the pan, brown lightly, then stir in the lemon rind, cider and stock and boil for about 3 minutes. Return all the pork to the pan and cook gently for about 25 minutes until the pork is tender.

Stir the apples into the pan and cook for a further 5 minutes. Using a slotted spoon, transfer the pork, onions and apples to a warmed serving dish, cover and keep warm. Add the parsley and stir the cream into the pan and allow to bubble to thicken the sauce slightly. Season, then pour over the pork and serve immediately.

cold desserts

Fabulous fruit, nutritious, colourful and brimming with
flavour, makes the best cold desserts. Enjoy a wide range
of dishes from simple creations such as Pears with
Honey and Wine, where one fruit stands alone in all
its glory, through classics like Summer Pudding, to
heavenly treats such as Raspberry and Nectarine Pavlova
and favourite combinations with a new twist like
Frozen Apple and Blackberry Terrine.

TROPICAL BANANA FRUIT SALAD

Not surprisingly, bananas go particularly well with other tropical fruits.

Serves 4–6

1 medium pineapple

400g/14oz can guava halves
*   in syrup*

1 large mango, peeled, stoned
*   and diced*

2 medium bananas

115g/4oz/⅔ cup stem ginger, plus
*   30ml/2 tbsp of the syrup*

60ml/4 tbsp thick coconut milk

10ml/2 tsp granulated sugar

2.5ml/½ tsp grated nutmeg

2.5ml/½ tsp ground cinnamon

strips of fresh coconut, to decorate

COOK'S TIP

For an appealing decorative touch, use two small pineapples. Cut them in half, through the leaves, carefully scoop out the pulp and use the shells as containers for the tropical fruit salad.

Peel the pineapple, remove the core, cut the flesh into cubes and place in a large serving bowl. Drain the guavas, reserving the syrup, and chop them into dice. Add the guavas and mango to the bowl. Slice one of the bananas and add it to the bowl.

Chop the stem ginger and add it to the pineapple mixture. Mix together lightly. Pour the ginger syrup into a blender or food processor. Add the reserved guava syrup, coconut milk and sugar. Slice the remaining banana and add to the mixture. Blend to a smooth, creamy purée.

Pour the banana and coconut purée over the fruit, add a little freshly grated nutmeg and a good sprinkling of the ground cinnamon. Serve the fruit salad chilled, decorated with strips of coconut.

WATERMELON, GINGER AND GRAPEFRUIT SALAD

The combination of fruit and ginger is very light and refreshing for a summer meal.

Serves 4

*500g/1¼lb/2 cups diced
    watermelon flesh*

2 ruby or pink grapefruit

2 pieces stem ginger in syrup

30ml/2 tbsp stem ginger syrup

COOK'S TIP

*Toss the fruits gently –
grapefruit segments will break
up easily and the appearance of
the dish will be spoiled.*

Remove any seeds from the watermelon and cut the flesh into bite-size chunks. Using a small sharp knife, cut away all the peel and white pith from the grapefruits and carefully lift out the segments. Work over a bowl to catch any juice. Finely chop the stem ginger and place in a serving bowl with the melon cubes and grapefruit segments, adding the reserved juice. Spoon the ginger syrup over the fruits and toss lightly together before serving.

GINGER AND HONEY WINTER FRUITS

A compote of dried fruit flavoured with honey is equally tasty as a dessert or breakfast dish. Serve it with lashings of Greek yogurt or cream.

Serves 4

1 lemon

4 green cardamom pods

1 cinnamon stick

150ml/¼ pint/⅔ cup clear honey

30ml/2 tbsp ginger syrup, from the jar

450g/1lb/2½ cups dried fruit salad

3 pieces of stem ginger

1 orange, peeled and segmented

VARIATION
Omit the ginger syrup and use 30ml/2 tbsp rosewater instead. Add 50g/2oz/½ cup blanched almonds as well.

Thinly pare 2 strips of rind from the lemon. Lightly crush the cardamom pods with the back of a heavy-bladed knife. Place the lemon rind, cardamoms, cinnamon stick, honey and ginger syrup in a heavy-based saucepan. Pour in 60ml/4 tbsp water and add the dried fruit. Bring to the boil, then lower the heat and simmer for 10 minutes. Pour into a serving bowl. Set aside until cool.

Chop the ginger and stir it into the fruit salad, with the orange segments. Cover and chill until ready to serve.

BLUEBERRY AND ORANGE SALAD WITH LAVENDER MERINGUES

Delicate blueberries and tangy oranges are combined with tiny lavender-flavoured meringues in this simple but stunning fruit salad. Lavender sprigs add the final decorative touch.

Serves 4

6 oranges

350g/12oz/3 cups blueberries

8 fresh lavender sprigs

For the meringue

2 egg whites

115g/4oz/1/2 cup caster sugar

5ml/1 tsp fresh lavender flowers

COOK'S TIP

Lavender is used in both sweet and savoury dishes. Always use fresh or recently dried flowers, and avoid artificially scented bunches that are sold for domestic purposes. Of course, if you can't find fresh lavender, then you could just make plain meringues instead.

Preheat the oven to 140°C/275°F/Gas 1. Line a baking tray with six layers of newspaper and cover with non-stick baking paper. Whisk the egg whites in a large mixing bowl until they hold soft peaks. Add the sugar a little at a time, whisking thoroughly after each addition until the meringue is thick and glossy, then fold in the lavender flowers.

Spoon the meringue into a piping bag fitted with a 5mm/1/4in plain nozzle. Pipe as many small buttons of meringue on to the prepared baking sheet as you can. Bake the meringues near the bottom of the oven for 1½–2 hours.

To segment the oranges, remove the peel from the top, bottom and sides with a serrated knife. Loosen the segments by cutting with a paring knife between the flesh and the membranes, holding the fruit over a bowl, then arrange the segments on four plates.

Combine the blueberries with the lavender meringues and pile in the centre of each plate. Decorate with sprigs of lavender and serve.

STRAWBERRIES WITH COINTREAU

Strawberries are one of summer's greatest pleasures. Try this simple way to serve them.

Serves 4

1 unwaxed orange

40g/1¹/₂oz/3 tbsp granulated sugar

75ml/5 tbsp water

45ml/3 tbsp Cointreau or
orange liqueur

450g/1lb/3 cups strawberries, hulled

250ml/8fl oz/1 cup whipping cream

VARIATION
Instead of using strawberries on their own in this dessert, add a mixture of other fresh seasonal berries, such as raspberries and blueberries, along with sliced summer fruits like peaches and nectarines.

Peel wide strips of rind without the pith from the orange and cut into very thin julienne strips. Combine the sugar and water in a small saucepan. Bring to the boil over a high heat, swirling the pan occasionally to dissolve the sugar. Add the julienne strips and simmer for 10 minutes. Remove the pan from the heat and leave the syrup to cool, then stir in the Cointreau.

Reserve four strawberries for decoration and cut the rest in halves or quarters. Put them in a bowl and pour the syrup and orange rind over the top. Set aside for 2 hours. Whip the cream and sweeten to taste. Serve the strawberries with cream and the reserved strawberries.

ICED PINEAPPLE CRUSH WITH STRAWBERRIES AND LYCHEES

The sweet tropical flavours of pineapple and lychees mixed with strawberries make this a refreshing salad.

Serves 4

2 small pineapples

450g/1lb/3 cups strawberries

400g/14oz can lychees

45ml/3 tbsp Kirsch or white rum

30ml/2 tbsp icing sugar

COOK'S TIP

A ripe pineapple will resist pressure when squeezed and will have a sweet, fragrant smell. In winter, freezing conditions can cause the flesh to blacken.

Remove the crown from both pineapples by twisting sharply. Reserve the leaves for decoration. Cut the fruit in half diagonally with a large serrated knife. Cut around the flesh inside the skin with a small serrated knife, keeping the skin intact. Remove the core from the pineapple.

Chop the pineapple and combine with the strawberries and lychees, taking care not to damage the fruit. Combine the Kirsch or white rum with the icing sugar, pour over the fruit and freeze for 45 minutes. Spoon the semi-frozen fruit into the pineapple skins and decorate with pineapple leaves.

MIXED FRUIT AND BERRY SALAD WITH COFFEE CREAM

The inspiration for this refreshing sweet salad came from Japan. Scented fruits and berries are mixed together and served with minted coffee cream, which is excellent with fresh fruit.

Serves 6

1 small fresh pineapple

2 large ripe pears

2 fresh peaches

12 strawberries

12 canned lychees and the juice from
  the can

6 small mint sprigs, plus extra sprigs
  to decorate

15ml/1 tbsp instant coffee granules

30ml/2 tbsp boiling water

150ml/¼ pint/⅔ cup double cream

VARIATION

Use fresh lychees when they are in season. Choose fruit with a pink or red skin which indicates that the lychee will be sweet and ripe. The skin is brittle and peels off easily and the fruit should be pearly white.

Peel and stone the fruit as necessary and chop into even-size pieces. Place all the fruit in a large glass bowl and pour on the lychee juice. Chill for at least an hour until ready to serve.

To make the sauce, remove the leaves from the mint sprigs and place them in a food processor or blender with the instant coffee granules and boiling water. Blend until smooth. Add the cream and process again briefly.

Serve the fruit salad decorated with small sprigs of mint, and hand the coffee sauce round separately.

BANANA AND MELON IN ORANGE VANILLA SAUCE

A chilled banana and melon compote in a delicious orange sauce makes a perfect summer dessert.

Serves 4

300ml/½ pint/1¼ cups orange juice

1 vanilla pod

5ml/1 tsp finely grated orange rind

15ml/1 tbsp granulated sugar

4 ripe but firm bananas

1 honeydew melon

30ml/2 tbsp lemon juice

strips of blanched orange rind, to
  garnish (optional)

COOK'S TIP

*Most large supermarkets and
health food shops sell vanilla
pods, and you can wash, dry
and store them for re-use. If
unavailable, use a few drops of
vanilla essence instead.*

Place the orange juice in a small saucepan with the vanilla pod, orange rind and sugar. Heat gently, stirring until the sugar has dissolved, then bring to the boil.

Lower the heat and simmer gently for 15 minutes or until the sauce is syrupy. Remove from the heat and leave to cool. Remove the vanilla pod. If using vanilla essence, stir it into the sauce once it has cooled.

Roughly chop the bananas and melon, place in a large serving bowl and toss with the lemon juice. Pour the cooled sauce over and chill the compote. Decorate with the blanched orange rind, if using, before serving.

RASPBERRY SALAD WITH MANGO CUSTARD SAUCE

This attractive salad unites the sharp quality of fresh raspberries and fragrant mango with two special sauces made from the same fruits.

Serves 4

1 large mango
3 egg yolks
30ml/2 tbsp caster sugar
10ml/2 tsp cornflour
200ml/7fl oz/scant 1 cup milk
8 fresh mint sprigs, to decorate

For the raspberry sauce
500g/1¼lb/3⅓ cups raspberries
45ml/3 tbsp caster sugar

COOK'S TIP
Mangoes are ripe when they yield to gentle pressure in the hand. Some varieties show a red-gold or yellow flush when they are ready to eat.

To prepare the mango, remove the top and bottom with a serrated knife. Cut away the outer skin, then remove the flesh by cutting either side of the flat central stone. Save one half of the fruit for decoration and roughly chop the rest of the flesh.

To make the custard, combine the egg yolks, sugar, cornflour and 30ml/2 tbsp of the milk smoothly in a bowl.

Rinse out a small saucepan with cold water to prevent the milk from catching. Bring the rest of the milk to the boil in the pan, pour it over the egg yolk mixture in the bowl and stir evenly.

Strain the mixture back into the saucepan. Cook over a low heat, stirring constantly, until it thickens enough to coat the back of the spoon.

Pour the custard into a food processor or blender, add the chopped mango and blend until smooth. Leave to cool.

To make the raspberry sauce, place 350g/12oz/2 cups of the raspberries in a stainless-steel saucepan. Add the sugar, soften over a gentle heat and simmer for 5 minutes. Using a wooden spoon, rub the fruit through a fine nylon sieve to remove the seeds. Leave to cool.

Spoon the raspberry sauce and mango custard into two pools on four plates. Slice the reserved mango and fan out or arrange in a pattern over the raspberry sauce. Scatter fresh raspberries over the mango custard. Decorate with mint sprigs and serve.

SUMMER BERRY SALAD WITH FRESH MANGO SAUCE

When you have only a few berries to hand, combine them with other summer fruits to make a colourful, refreshing fruit salad. Serve it simply with cream or ice cream, or drizzle with a vibrant mango sauce.

Serves 6

*1 large ripe mango, peeled, stoned
  and chopped*
rind of 1 unwaxed orange
juice of 3 oranges
caster sugar, to taste
2 peaches
2 nectarines
1 small mango, peeled
2 plums
1 pear or ½ small melon
juice of 1 lemon
*25–50g/1–2oz/2 heaped tbsp wild
  strawberries (optional)*
*25–50g/1–2oz/2 heaped tbsp
  raspberries*
*25–50g/1–2oz/2 heaped tbsp
  blueberries*
small mint sprigs, to decorate

In a food processor fitted with the metal blade, process the large mango until smooth. Add the orange rind, juice and sugar to taste and process again until very smooth. Press through a sieve into a bowl and chill the sauce.

Peel the peaches, if liked, then slice and stone the peaches, nectarines, small mango and plums. Quarter the pear and remove the core and seeds, or, if using, slice the melon thinly and remove the peel.

Place the sliced fruits on a large plate, sprinkle the fruits with the lemon juice and chill, covered with clear film, for up to 3 hours before serving. (Some fruits may discolour if cut too far ahead of time.)

To serve, arrange the sliced fruits on serving plates, spoon the berries on top, drizzle with a little mango sauce and decorate with mint sprigs. Serve the remaining sauce separately.

STRAWBERRIES WITH RASPBERRY AND PASSION FRUIT SAUCE

Strawberries release their finest flavour when served with raspberry and passion fruit sauce.

Serves 4

*350g/12oz/2 cups raspberries, fresh
    or frozen*

45ml/3 tbsp caster sugar

2 passion fruits

700g/1½lb/4 cups small strawberries

8 plain finger biscuits, to serve

Place the raspberries and sugar in a saucepan and cook over a low heat, stirring occasionally, until simmering. Cook gently for 5 minutes, then leave to cool. Halve the passion fruits and scoop out the seeds and juice. Pour the raspberries into a blender or food processor, add the passion fruit pulp and blend for a few seconds.

Rub the fruit sauce through a fine nylon sieve to remove the seeds. Fold the strawberries into the sauce, then spoon into four stemmed glasses. Serve with plain finger biscuits.

COOK'S TIP

When buying strawberries, choose fruit that is brightly coloured, firm and unblemished. For the best flavour, serve the berries at room temperature. The delicate flavour will then be at its most intense.

FIG AND PEAR COMPOTE WITH RASPBERRIES

A simple yet sophisticated dessert featuring succulent, ripe autumnal fruits, enhanced by tangy raspberries.

Serves 4

75g/3oz/6 tbsp caster sugar

1 bottle red wine

1 vanilla pod, split

1 strip pared lemon rind

4 pears

2 purple figs, quartered

225g/8oz/1⅓ cups fresh raspberries

lemon juice, to taste

Put the sugar and wine in a large pan and heat gently until dissolved. Add the vanilla pod and lemon rind and bring to the boil. Simmer for 5 minutes. Peel and halve the pears, then scoop out the cores, using a melon baller. Add the pears to the syrup and poach for 15 minutes, turning the pears several times so they colour evenly. Add the figs and poach for a further 5 minutes, until the fruits are tender. Transfer the poached fruit to a serving bowl using a slotted spoon, then scatter over the raspberries.

Return the syrup to the heat and boil rapidly to reduce slightly. Add a little lemon juice to taste. Strain over the fruits and serve warm.

PEARS WITH HONEY AND WINE

California produces several types of honey, the best known being sage blossom and alfalfa. In this California recipe, honey sweetens a mulled wine mixture used for stewing pears.

Serves 4

1 bottle of red Zinfandel wine

175g/6oz/¾ cup granulated sugar

45ml/3 tbsp clear honey

juice of ½ lemon

1 cinnamon stick

1 vanilla pod, split open lengthways,
*   or a few drops of vanilla essence*

5cm/2in piece of pared orange rind

1 whole clove

1 black peppercorn

4 firm ripe pears

whipped cream or soured cream,
*   to serve*

In a saucepan just large enough to hold the pears standing upright, combine the wine, sugar, honey, lemon juice, cinnamon stick, vanilla pod or essence, orange rind, clove and peppercorn. Heat gently, stirring occasionally until the sugar has dissolved.

Meanwhile, peel the pears, leaving the core and stem intact on each. Slice a small piece off the base of each pear so that it will stand upright, then gently place the pears in the wine mixture. Simmer the pears uncovered, for 20–35 minutes, depending on size and ripeness. They should be just tender; do not overcook.

With a slotted spoon, gently transfer the pears to a bowl. Continue to boil the poaching liquid until reduced by about half. Leave to cool, then strain over the pears. Chill for at least 3 hours.

Place the pears in serving dishes and spoon over the chilled wine syrup. Serve with whipped cream or soured cream.

COOK'S TIP
Choose pears of similar size and shape for this attractive hot dessert.

FRUDITÉS WITH HONEY DIP

Some of the simplest desserts are also the most delectable. This takes only minutes to make but tastes absolutely wonderful, making use of the classic honey and yogurt combination.

Serves 4

250ml/8fl oz/1 cup thick natural
   yogurt
45ml/3 tbsp clear honey
selection of fresh fruit for dipping
   (such as apples, pears, tangerines,
   grapes, figs, cherries, strawberries
   and kiwi fruit)

VARIATION
Add a few langues de chat *or other dessert biscuits, such as sponge fingers, to the platter. Children like the yogurt dip served on its own, with sliced bananas stirred in.*

Place the yogurt in a dish, beat until smooth, then stir in the honey, swirling it to create a marbled effect.

Cut the fruit into wedges or bite-size pieces, or leave whole.

Arrange the selection of fruits on a platter with the bowl of dip in the centre. Serve chilled.

BRAZILIAN COFFEE BANANAS

Rich, lavish and sinful-looking, this banana dessert takes only moments to make.

Serves 4

4 small ripe bananas

15ml/1 tbsp instant coffee granules or powder

30ml/2 tbsp dark muscovado sugar

250g/9oz/generous 1 cup Greek-style yogurt

15ml/1 tbsp toasted flaked almonds

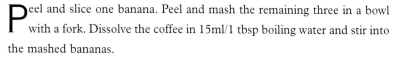

Peel and slice one banana. Peel and mash the remaining three in a bowl with a fork. Dissolve the coffee in 15ml/1 tbsp boiling water and stir into the mashed bananas.

Spoon a little of the mashed banana mixture into four serving dishes and sprinkle with sugar. Top with a spoonful of yogurt, then repeat the layers until all the ingredients are used up.

Using a skewer or cocktail stick, swirl the last layer of yogurt for a marbled effect. Finish with a few banana slices and flaked almonds. Serve cold, preferably within an hour of making.

VARIATION

For a special occasion, add a dash of dark rum, brandy or crème de cacao to the bananas for extra richness.

APPLE FOAM WITH BLACKBERRIES

Any seasonal soft fruit can be used for this delicious dessert if blackberries are not available at the time.

Serves 4

225g/8oz/2 cups blackberries

150ml/¼ pint/⅔ cup apple juice

5ml/1 tsp powdered gelatine

15ml/1 tbsp clear honey

2 egg whites

COOK'S TIP

Make sure that you add the gelatine to a cold liquid before dissolving over a very low heat. Gelatine must not boil, or it will lose its setting ability. Once set, gelatine mixtures should be left in the fridge for about 2 hours to become firm. Don't be tempted to chill a gelatine mixture quickly in the freezer, as it tends to crystallize and separate.

Place the blackberries in a pan with 60ml/4 tbsp of the apple juice and heat gently until the fruit is soft. Remove from the heat, cool and chill.

Sprinkle the gelatine over the remaining apple juice in a small pan and stir over a low heat until dissolved. Stir in the honey.

Whisk the egg whites until they hold stiff peaks. Continue whisking hard and pour in the hot gelatine mixture gradually, until well mixed.

Quickly spoon the foam into rough mounds on individual plates. Chill. Serve with the blackberries and juice spooned around.

PEACHES WITH RASPBERRY SAUCE

Escoffier created this dessert, known as Peach Melba, in honour of the opera singer Nellie Melba.

Serves 6

1 litre/1³/4 pints/4 cups water

50g/2oz/¹/4 cup caster sugar

1 vanilla pod, split lengthways

3 large peaches, halved and stoned

For the raspberry sauce

*450g/1lb/2¹/2 cups fresh or
  frozen raspberries*

15ml/1 tbsp lemon juice

25–40g/1–1¹/2oz/2–3 tbsp caster sugar

*30–45ml/2–3 tbsp raspberry
  liqueur (optional)*

vanilla ice cream, to serve

mint leaves, to decorate

COOK'S TIP

*Prepare the peaches and sauce
up to one day in advance. Leave
the peaches in the syrup and
cover them and the sauce
before chilling.*

In a large saucepan, combine the water, sugar and vanilla pod. Bring to the boil, stirring to dissolve the sugar. Add the peaches, cut-sides down, with water, if needed, to cover the fruit. Press a piece of greaseproof paper against the surface, then cover and simmer for 12–15 minutes until tender. Remove the pan from the heat and leave the peaches to cool. Peel the peaches.

Whiz the raspberries, lemon juice and sugar in a food processor for 1 minute, then sieve into a bowl. Add the raspberry liqueur, if using, and chill. To serve, place a peach half, cut-side up, add vanilla ice cream and spoon over the raspberry sauce. Decorate with mint leaves.

FRESH RASPBERRY AND PASSION FRUIT CHINCHILLA SOUFFLES

Few desserts are as easy to make as this one: beaten egg whites and sugar, combined with passion fruits, are baked in a dish, turned out and served with a handful of raspberries.

Serves 4

25g/1oz/2 tbsp butter, softened

5 egg whites

150g/5oz/²⁄₃ cup caster sugar

2 passion fruits

250ml/8fl oz/1 cup ready-made custard from a carton or can

milk, as required

675g/1¹⁄₂lb/4 cups fresh raspberries

icing sugar, for dusting

Preheat the oven to 180°C/350°F/Gas 4. Brush four 300ml/½ pint/1¼ cup soufflé dishes with a visible layer of soft butter.

Whisk the egg whites in a mixing bowl until firm. (You can use an electric whisk.) Add the sugar a little at a time and whisk into a firm meringue.

Halve the passion fruits, take out the seeds with a spoon and fold them into the meringue.

Spoon the meringue into the prepared dishes, stand in a deep roasting tin which has been half-filled with boiling water and bake for 10 minutes. The meringue will rise above the tops of the soufflé dishes.

Turn the chinchillas out upside-down on to serving plates. Thin the custard with a little milk and pour around the edge.

Top with raspberries, dredge with icing sugar and serve warm or cold.

VARIATION

If raspberries are out of season, use either fresh, bottled or canned soft fruit such as strawberries, blueberries, blackberries or redcurrants.

FLUFFY BANANA AND PINEAPPLE MOUSSE

This light, low-fat banana mousse looks very impressive but is extremely easy to make.

Serves 6

2 ripe bananas

225g/8oz/1 cup cottage cheese

425g/15oz can pineapple chunks or
pieces in juice

15ml/1 tbsp/1 sachet powdered
gelatine

2 egg whites

COOK'S TIP

For a simpler way of serving,
use a 1-litre/1³/4-pint/4-cup
serving dish, which will hold
all the mixture, and do not tie
a collar around the edge.
Decorate the top with the
reserved banana and pineapple
as described in the recipe.

Tie a double band of non-stick baking paper around a 600-ml/1-pint/2½-cup soufflé dish to come 5cm/2in above the rim. Peel and chop one banana and place it in a food processor with the cottage cheese. Process until smooth.

Drain the pineapple, saving the juice and setting aside a few pieces for decoration. Add the rest of the pineapple to the mixture in the processor and process for a few seconds until finely chopped.

Pour 60ml/4 tbsp of the reserved pineapple juice into a small heatproof bowl and sprinkle the gelatine on top. When spongy, place over simmering water, stirring until the gelatine has dissolved. Stir the gelatine quickly into the fruit mixture. Whisk the egg whites to soft peaks. Fold them into the mixture. Tip the mousse mixture into the prepared dish, smooth the surface and chill until set. Carefully remove the paper collar. Slice the remaining banana and use it with the reserved pineapple to decorate the mousse.

MANGO AND GINGER CLOUDS

*The sweet, perfumed flavour of ripe mango combines beautifully with ginger, and this low-fat dessert
makes the very most of them both.*

Serves 6

3 ripe mangoes

3 pieces stem ginger in syrup

45ml/3 tbsp stem ginger syrup

75g/3oz/¹/₂ cup silken tofu

3 egg whites

6 pistachios, chopped

Cut the mangoes in half and remove the stones. Peel and roughly chop the flesh. Put the mango flesh in a blender or food processor with the ginger, syrup and tofu. Blend until smooth. Spoon into a bowl. Put the egg whites in a bowl and whisk them until they form soft peaks. Fold the egg whites lightly into the mango mixture.

Spoon the mixture into wide dishes or glasses and chill well before serving, sprinkled with the chopped pistachios.

VARIATION

*If you prefer, you can serve this
dessert lightly frozen. Add the
nuts just before serving.*

COOK'S TIP

*Don't serve raw egg whites
to pregnant women, babies,
young children, the elderly,
or anyone who is ill.*

GRAPE AND HONEY WHIP

Frosted grapes add the finishing touches to this simple dessert, which is sweetened with clear honey.

Serves 4

115g/4oz/1 cup black or green
*   seedless grapes, plus 4 sprigs*
2 egg whites
15ml/1 tbsp granulated sugar
finely grated rind and juice of
*   ½ lemon*
250g/9oz/1 cup cream cheese
45ml/3 tbsp clear honey
30ml/2 tbsp brandy (optional)

VARIATION
Instead of brandy, use a honey-
based liqueur such as Irish
Mist, made from Irish whiskey,
heather honey and herbs.

Brush the sprigs of grapes lightly with some of the egg whites and sprinkle with sugar to coat. Leave to dry.

Pour the lemon juice into a bowl and stir in the rind, cheese, honey and brandy, if using. Chop the remaining grapes and stir them in.

Whisk the remaining egg whites until they are stiff enough to hold soft peaks. Fold them into the grape mixture, then spoon into serving glasses. Top with the sugar-frosted grapes and serve chilled.

RASPBERRY AND PASSION FRUIT SWIRLS

If passion fruits are not available, this simple low-fat dessert can be made with raspberries alone.

Serves 4

300g/11oz/scant 2 cups raspberries

2 passion fruits

*400g/14oz/1⅔ cups low-fat
   fromage frais*

30ml/2 tbsp caster sugar

raspberries and mint sprigs, to decorate

Mash the raspberries in a small bowl with a fork until the juice runs. Scoop out the passion fruit pulp into a separate bowl with the fromage frais and sugar and mix well.

Spoon alternate spoonfuls of the raspberry pulp and the fromage frais mixture into stemmed glasses or one large serving dish, stirring lightly to create a swirled effect.

Decorate each dessert with a whole raspberry and a fresh mint sprig. Chill until ready to serve.

COOK'S TIP
*Over-ripe, slightly soft fruit can
also be used in this recipe. Use
frozen raspberries when fresh
are not available, but thaw
them first.*

QUICK BANANA PUDDING

For instant energy and excellent taste, tuck into this simple banana pudding with a caramel topping.

Serves 6–8

4 thick slices of ginger cake

6 ripe bananas

30ml/2 tbsp lemon juice

300ml/½ pint/1¼ cups
   whipping cream

60ml/4 tbsp orange juice

30–45ml/2–3 tbsp soft light
   brown sugar

VARIATION

You could use fromage frais instead of whipping cream if you prefer. However, do not try to whip it – simply stir in half the recommended amount of fruit juice.

Break up the cake into chunks and arrange in an ovenproof dish. Slice the bananas into a bowl and toss with the lemon juice.

Whip the cream in a separate bowl until firm, then gently whip in the juice. Fold in the bananas and spoon the mixture over the ginger cake.

Top with the sugar, sprinkling it in an even layer. Place under a hot grill for 2–3 minutes to caramelize. Chill in the refrigerator until set firm again, if you wish, or serve at once.

BANANA AND PASSION FRUIT WHIP

Creamy mashed bananas combine beautifully with passion fruit in this easy and quickly prepared dessert.

Serves 4

2 ripe bananas

2 passion fruit

90ml/6 tbsp fromage frais

150ml/¼ pint/⅔ cup double cream

10ml/2 tsp clear honey

shortcake or ginger biscuits, to serve

COOK'S TIP
Look out for cans of passion fruit (or grenadilla) pulp. Use with sliced banana and whipped cream to make a marvellous topping for pavlova or for sandwiching together individual meringues.

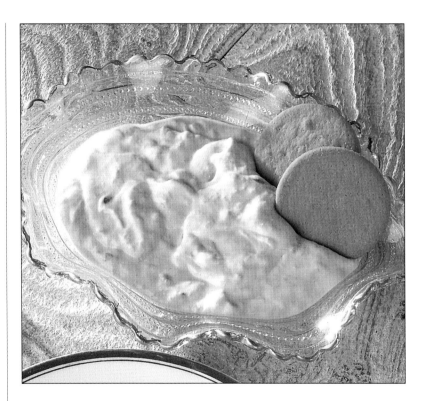

Slice the bananas into a bowl then, using a fork, mash them to a smooth purée. Cut the passion fruit in half. Using a teaspoon, scoop the pulp into the bowl. Add the fromage frais and mix gently.

In a separate bowl, whip the cream with the honey until it forms soft peaks. Carefully fold the cream and honey mixture into the fruit. Spoon into four glass dishes and serve the whip at once, with the biscuits.

BLACKBERRY AND APPLE ROMANOFF

Rich yet fruity, this dessert is popular with most people and very quick to make.

Serves 6–8

3–4 sharp eating apples, peeled, cored
   and chopped
45ml/3 tbsp caster sugar
250ml/8fl oz/1 cup whipping cream
5ml/1 tsp grated lemon rind
90ml/6 tbsp Greek-style yogurt
4–6 crisp meringues (about 50g/2oz),
   roughly crumbled
225g/8oz/2 cups fresh or
   frozen blackberries
whipped cream, a few blackberries and
   mint leaves, to decorate

COOK'S TIP
*You can also make this into a
delicious ice cream, though the
texture of the frozen berries
makes it difficult to scoop if it is
frozen for more than 4–6 hours.*

With clear film, line a 900ml/1½ pint/3¾ cup pudding basin. Toss the apples into a pan with 30ml/2 tbsp sugar and cook for 2–3 minutes, or until softening. Mash with a fork and leave to cool.

Whip the cream and fold in the lemon rind, yogurt, the remaining sugar, the apples and the crumbled meringues.

Gently stir in the blackberries, then tip the mixture into the pudding basin and freeze for 1–3 hours.

Turn out on to a plate and remove the clear film. Serve decorated with piped cream, blackberries and mint leaves.

BANANA HONEY YOGURT ICE

Smooth and silky, this delicious banana ice is very refreshing when eaten after a rich meal.

Serves 4-6

4 ripe bananas, roughly chopped

15ml/1 tbsp lemon juice

30ml/2 tbsp clear honey

*250g/9oz/generous 1 cup Greek-
  style yogurt*

2.5ml/½ tsp ground cinnamon

*crisp biscuits, flaked hazelnuts and
  banana slices, to serve*

Place the bananas in a food processor or blender with the lemon juice, honey, yogurt and cinnamon. Process until smooth and creamy.

Pour the mixture into a suitable container for freezing and freeze until almost solid. Spoon back into the food processor and process the mixture again until smooth.

Return the yogurt ice to the freezer until firm. Before serving, allow the ice to soften at room temperature for 15 minutes. Scoop into individual bowls and serve with crisp biscuits, flaked hazelnuts and banana slices.

COOK'S TIP
Switch the freezer to the coldest setting about an hour before making the yogurt ice to ensure that it freezes quickly.

BREAD AND BANANA YOGURT ICE

Serve this tempting yogurt ice with strawberries and biscuits for a luscious, light dessert.

Serves 6

115g/4oz/2 cups fresh
    wholemeal breadcrumbs
50g/2oz/⅓ cup soft light brown sugar
300ml/½ pint/1¾ cups ready-made
    cold custard
150g/5oz fromage frais
150ml/¼ pint/⅔ cup Greek-
    style yogurt
4 bananas
juice of 1 lemon
25g/1oz/¼ cup icing sugar, sifted
50g/2oz/½ cup raisins, chopped
pared lemon rind, to decorate
fresh strawberries, halved, to serve

COOK'S TIP

Transfer the ice to the refrigerator about 30 minutes before serving to allow it to soften a little. This will make it easier to scoop neatly so that it looks attractive when served.

Preheat the oven to 200°C/400°F/Gas 6. Mix the breadcrumbs and brown sugar in a bowl. Spread the mixture out on a non-stick baking sheet. Bake for about 10 minutes until the crumbs are crisp, stirring occasionally. Set aside to cool.

Meanwhile, mix the custard, fromage frais and yogurt in a bowl. Mash the bananas with the lemon juice and add to the custard mixture, mixing well. Fold in the icing sugar.

Pour the mixture into a shallow, freezerproof container and freeze for about 3 hours or until mushy in consistency. Spoon into a chilled bowl and quickly mash with a fork to break down the ice crystals.

Add the breadcrumbs and raisins and mix well. Return the mixture to the container, cover and freeze until firm. Serve with the strawberries, if using, decorated with lemon rind.

FROZEN APPLE AND BLACKBERRY TERRINE

Apples and blackberries are a classic autumn combination; they really complement each other. This pretty, three-layered terrine can be frozen, so you can enjoy it at any time of year.

Serves 6

*2 cooking or eating apples (about
  450g/1lb)*
300ml/½ pint/1¼ cups sweet cider
15ml/1 tbsp clear honey
5ml/1 tsp vanilla essence
*200g/7oz/scant 2 cups fresh or frozen
  blackberries, thawed*
15ml/1 tbsp/1 sachet powdered gelatine
2 egg whites
*fresh apple slices and blackberries,
  to decorate*

COOK'S TIP

For a quicker version, set the mixture without layering. Purée the fruit, stir the dissolved gelatine and whisked egg whites into the mixture, turn into the tin and leave to set.

Peel, core and chop the apples and place them in a pan, with half the cider. Bring the cider to the boil, and then cover the pan and let the apples simmer gently until tender.

Tip the apples into a food processor or blender and process them to a smooth purée. Stir in the honey and vanilla. Add half the blackberries to half the apple purée, and then process again until smooth. Sieve the purée to remove the blackberry pips.

Heat the remaining cider until it is almost boiling, and then sprinkle the gelatine over and stir until the gelatine has completely dissolved. Add half the gelatine mixture to the apple purée and half to the blackberry purée.

Leave the purées to cool until almost set. Whisk the egg whites until they are stiff. Quickly fold them into the apple purée. Remove half the purée to another bowl. Stir the remaining whole blackberries into half the apple purée, and then tip this into a 1.75 litre/3 pint/7½ cup loaf tin.

Top with the blackberry purée and spread it evenly. Finally, add a layer of the apple purée and smooth it evenly. If necessary, freeze each layer until firm before adding the next.

Freeze until firm. To serve, allow to stand at room temperature for about 20 minutes to soften, and then cut in slices, decorated with the fresh apple slices and blackberries.

MINT AND LEMON SORBET

This sorbet has a very refreshing, delicate taste, perfect for a hot afternoon.

Serves 6–8

450g/1lb/2 cups sugar

475ml/16fl oz/2 cups water

6 mint sprigs, plus more to decorate

6 lemon balm leaves

250ml/8fl oz/1 cup dry white wine

30ml/2 tbsp lemon juice

dill sprigs, to decorate

Place the sugar and water in a saucepan with the washed herbs. Bring to the boil. Remove from the heat and add the wine. Cover and cool. Chill for several hours, then add the lemon juice. Freeze in a suitable container. As soon as the mixture begins to freeze, stir it briskly and replace in the freezer. Repeat every 15 minutes for at least 3 hours or until ready to serve.

To make the small ice bowls, pour about 1cm/½in cold, boiled water into small freezer-proof bowls, about 600ml/1 pint/2½ cups in capacity, and arrange some herbs in the water. Place in the freezer. Once this has frozen add a little more water to cover the herbs and freeze.

Place a smaller freezer-proof bowl inside each larger bowl and put a heavy weight inside, such as a metal weight from some scales. Fill between the bowls with more cooled boiled water, float more herbs in this and freeze.

To release the ice bowls, warm the inner bowl with a small amount of very hot water and twist it out. Warm the outer bowl by standing it in very hot water for a few seconds, then tip out the ice bowl. Spoon the sorbet into the ice bowls, decorate with mint and dill sprigs and serve.

COOK'S TIP

Instead of lemon balm leaves,
fresh flowers can be used in the
ice bowl. Small pansies,
marigolds or geraniums would
all be suitable.

BLACKBERRY SALAD WITH ROSE GRANITA

Blackberries combine especially well with rose water. Here a rose syrup is frozen into a granita and served over strips of white meringue.

Serves 4

150g/5oz/⅔ cup caster sugar
1 fresh red rose, petals finely chopped
5ml/1 tsp rose water
10ml/2 tsp lemon juice
450g/1lb/4 cups blackberries
icing sugar, for dusting

For the meringue
2 egg whites
115g/4oz/½ cup caster sugar

COOK'S TIP

Blackberries are widely cultivated from late spring to autumn and are usually juicy, plump and sweet. The finest berries have a slightly bitter edge and a strong depth of flavour. They are best appreciated with a light sprinkling of sugar.

Bring 150ml/¼ pint/⅔ cup water to the boil in a stainless-steel or enamel saucepan. Add the sugar and rose petals, then simmer for 5 minutes. Strain the syrup into a deep metal tray, add a further 450ml/¾ pint/scant 1⅞ cups water, the rose water and lemon juice, and leave to cool. Freeze the mixture for 3 hours or until solid.

Preheat the oven to 140°C/275°F/Gas 1. Line a baking sheet with six layers of newspaper and cover with non-stick baking paper.

To make the meringue, whisk the egg whites until they hold soft peaks. Add the caster sugar a little at a time and whisk until firm.

Spoon the meringue into a piping bag fitted with a 1cm/½in plain nozzle. Pipe the meringue in lengths across the paper-lined baking sheet. Bake in the bottom of the oven for 1½–2 hours.

Break the meringue into 5cm/2in lengths and place three or four lengths on each of four large plates. Pile the blackberries next to the meringue. With a tablespoon, scrape the granita finely. Shape into ovals and place over the meringue. Dust with icing sugar and serve.

LEMON MERINGUE BOMBE WITH MINT CHOCOLATE

This unusual ice cream has quite the most delicious combination of tastes that you can imagine.

Serves 6–8

2 large lemons

150g/5oz/⅔ cup granulated sugar

150ml/¼ pint/⅔ cup whipping cream

600ml/1 pint/2½ cups Greek natural yogurt

2 large meringues, roughly crushed

3 small mint sprigs

225g/8oz good-quality mint chocolate, grated

Remove the rind from the lemons with a vegetable peeler, then squeeze the juice. Place the lemon rind and sugar in a blender or food processor and blend finely. Add the cream, yogurt and lemon juice and process thoroughly. Pour the mixture into a mixing bowl and add the meringues.

Reserve one of the mint sprigs and chop the rest finely. Add to the cream and lemon mixture. Pour into a 1.2 litre/2 pint/5 cup glass pudding bowl and freeze for 4 hours.

When the ice cream has frozen, scoop out the middle and pour in the grated mint chocolate, reserving a little for the garnish. Replace the ice cream to cover the chocolate and refreeze.

To unmould, dip the bowl in very hot water for a few seconds to loosen the ice cream, then invert the bowl over a serving plate. Decorate with grated chocolate and a mint sprig.

COOK'S TIP

If you prefer, use either milk or plain chocolate instead of mint chocolate. To make a richer ice cream, use cream instead of the Greek yogurt.

COFFEE, PEACH AND ALMOND DAQUOISE

This is a traditional meringue gâteau, filled with a rich coffee buttercream and layered with peaches.

Serves 12

5 egg whites

275g/10oz/1¼ cups caster sugar

15g/½oz/2 tbsp cornflour

175g/6oz/1½ cups ground almonds,
*   toasted*

For the custard

5 egg yolks

150g/5oz/¾ cup caster sugar

125ml/4½fl oz/generous ½ cup milk

275g/10oz/1¼ cups unsalted butter,
*   diced*

45–60ml/3–4 tbsp coffee essence

2 × 400g/14oz cans peach halves,
*   drained and chopped, 3 halves*
*   reserved for decoration*

icing sugar, for dusting

toasted flaked almonds and a few
*   mint leaves, to decorate*

Preheat the oven to 150°C/300°F/Gas 2 and draw three 23cm/9in circles on to three sheets of non-stick baking paper. Place each on a separate baking sheet. Whisk the egg whites until stiff and gradually add the sugar, whisking until the mixture is thick and glossy. Fold in the cornflour and ground almonds. Spoon the mixture into a piping bag fitted with a plain nozzle and pipe in a continuous tight coil on to each prepared piece of baking paper, starting at the centre and gradually filling the circle. Bake for 1¾–2 hours until lightly golden and dried out. Peel away the paper and cool on a wire rack.

Make the custard: whisk the egg yolks with the sugar until thick and pale. Heat the milk in a pan until nearly boiling and pour over the egg mixture. Return the mixture to the pan and cook gently until just thickened. Cool slightly and strain into a bowl. Beat in the butter a little at a time until thickened and stir in the coffee essence.

Trim the meringue neatly, crushing any trimmings. Fold the chopped peaches and meringue trimmings into half of the custard and use this to sandwich the meringue circles together. Coat the top and sides of the meringue with the remaining custard and decorate with toasted almond flakes. Dust with icing sugar and finish with fans of the reserved peaches and a few mint leaves.

RASPBERRY MERINGUE GATEAU

A crisp, rich, hazelnut meringue filled with whipped cream and raspberries makes a wonderful dessert served with a fresh raspberry and orange sauce.

Serves 6

4 egg whites

225g/8oz/1 cup caster sugar

few drops vanilla essence

5ml/1 tsp distilled malt vinegar

115g/4oz/1 cup roasted and chopped
  hazelnuts, ground

300ml/½ pint/1¼ cups double cream

350g/12oz/2 cups raspberries

icing sugar, for dusting

raspberries and mint sprigs, to decorate

For the sauce

225g/8oz/1⅓ cups raspberries

45–60ml/3–4 tbsp icing sugar, sifted

15ml/1 tbsp orange liqueur

Preheat the oven to 180°C/350°F/Gas 4. Grease two 20cm/8in sandwich tins and line the bases with greaseproof paper.

Whisk the egg whites in a large bowl until they hold stiff peaks, then gradually whisk in the caster sugar a tablespoon at a time, whisking well after each addition to create a smooth mixture.

Continue whisking the meringue mixture for a minute or two until very stiff, then fold in the vanilla essence, vinegar and ground hazelnuts.

Divide the meringue mixture between the prepared sandwich tins and spread level. Bake for 50–60 minutes, until crisp. Remove the meringues from the tins and leave to cool on a wire rack.

While the meringues are cooling, make the sauce. Purée the raspberries with the icing sugar and orange liqueur in a blender or food processor, then press the purée through a fine nylon sieve to remove any pips. Chill the sauce until ready to serve.

Whip the cream until it forms soft peaks, then gently fold in the raspberries. Sandwich the meringue rounds together with the raspberry cream. Dust the top of the gâteau with icing sugar. Decorate with raspberries and mint sprigs and serve with the raspberry sauce.

VARIATION
Fresh redcurrants make a good alternative to raspberries. Add to the cream with a little sugar.

BLACKBERRY BROWN SUGAR MERINGUE

Brown sugar gives this meringue a delicate, fudge-like flavour which combines well with the berry filling.

Serves 6

175g/6oz/1 cup soft light brown sugar

3 egg whites

5ml/1 tsp distilled malt vinegar

2.5ml/½ tsp vanilla essence

For the filling

350–450g/12oz–1lb/3–4 cups
  blackberries

30ml/2 tbsp crème de cassis

300ml/½ pint/1¼ cups double cream

15ml/1 tbsp icing sugar, sifted

small blackberry leaves, to
  decorate (optional)

Preheat the oven to 160°C/325°F/Gas 3. Draw a 20cm/8in circle on a sheet of non-stick baking paper, turn over and place on a baking sheet.

Spread out the brown sugar on another baking sheet and dry in the oven for 8–10 minutes. Sieve to remove any lumps.

Whisk the egg whites in a bowl until stiff. Add half the dried brown sugar, 15ml/1 tbsp at a time, whisking well after each addition. Add the vinegar and vanilla essence, then fold in the remaining sugar.

Spoon the meringue on to the drawn circle on the paper, making a hollow in the centre. Bake for 45 minutes, then turn off the oven and leave the meringue in the oven with the door slightly open, until cold.

Place the blackberries in a bowl, sprinkle over the crème de cassis and leave to macerate for 30 minutes.

When the meringue is cold, carefully peel off the non-stick baking paper and transfer the meringue to a serving plate. Lightly whip the cream with the icing sugar and spoon into the centre. Top with the blackberries and decorate with small blackberry leaves, if liked. Serve at once.

RASPBERRY AND NECTARINE PAVLOVA

This meringue cake was created in the 1920s for the ballerina Anna Pavlova, when she visited Australia.

Serves 4–6

3 egg whites

175g/6oz/³⁄4 cup caster sugar

5ml/1 tsp cornflour

5ml/1 tsp white wine vinegar

*40g/1¹⁄2oz/5 tbsp chopped
roasted hazelnuts*

250ml/8fl oz/1 cup double cream

15ml/1 tbsp orange juice

*30ml/2 tbsp natural thick and
creamy yogurt*

2 ripe nectarines, stoned and sliced

225g/8oz/1¹⁄3 cups raspberries, halved

*15–30ml/1–2 tbsp redcurrant
jelly, warmed*

Preheat the oven to 140°C/275°F/Gas 1. Lightly grease a baking sheet. Draw a 20cm/8in circle on a sheet of non-stick baking paper. Place pencil-side down on the baking sheet.

Put the egg whites in a clean, grease-free bowl and whisk with an electric mixer until stiff. Whisk in the sugar, 15ml/1 tbsp at a time, whisking well after each addition. Add the cornflour, vinegar and hazelnuts and fold in carefully with a large metal spoon. Spoon the meringue on to the marked circle and spread out to the edges, making a dip in the centre. Bake for about 1¹⁄4–1¹⁄2 hours, until crisp. Leave to cool completely and transfer to a serving platter. Whip the cream and orange juice until just thick, stir in the yogurt and spoon on to the meringue. Top with the fruit and drizzle over the redcurrant jelly. Serve immediately.

HONEY AND MANGO CHEESECAKE

Use a fragrant citrus honey to complement the mango and lime in this exotic cheesecake.

Serves 4

40g/1½oz/3 tbsp butter or
  margarine, softened
30ml/2 tbsp clear honey
225g/8oz/2 cups oatmeal
1 large ripe mango, peeled, stoned
  and roughly chopped
275g/10oz/1¼ cups cream cheese
175ml/6fl oz/¾ cup natural yogurt
finely grated rind of 1 small lime
45ml/3 tbsp apple juice
20ml/4 tsp powdered gelatine
fresh mango and lime slices, to
  decorate

VARIATION

*Use drained canned mango
slices instead of fresh, if you
prefer, but add a few drops of
fresh lime juice to counteract
the sweetness.*

Preheat the oven to 200°C/400°F/Gas 6. Cream the butter or margarine with the honey in a bowl, then stir in the oatmeal. Press the mixture into the base of a 20cm/8in loose-bottomed cake tin. Bake for 12–15 minutes, until lightly browned. Cool.

Place the chopped mango, cheese, yogurt and lime rind in a food processor or blender and process until smooth.

Put the apple juice in a small heatproof bowl and sprinkle the gelatine on top. When spongy, set over simmering water and stir until the gelatine has dissolved. Stir into the cheese mixture.

Pour the filling over the cheesecake base and chill until set, then remove from the tin and place on a serving plate. Decorate the top with the mango and lime slices.

LEMON CHEESECAKE ON BRANDY SNAPS

Using ready-made brandy snaps gives a quick and crunchy golden base to this simple and delicious classic lemon cheesecake.

Serves 8

½ × 142g/4¾oz packet lemon jelly
450g/1lb/2 cups low-fat cream cheese
10ml/2 tsp lemon rind
75–115g/3–4oz/about ½ cup caster
  sugar
few drops vanilla essence
150ml/¼ pint/⅔ cup Greek-style
  yogurt
8 brandy snaps
mint leaves and icing sugar, to decorate

Dissolve the jelly in 45–60ml/3–4 tbsp boiling water in a heatproof measuring jug and, when clear, add sufficient cold water to make up to 150ml/¼ pint/⅔ cup. Chill until beginning to thicken. Line a 450g/1lb loaf tin with clear film.

Cream the cheese with the lemon rind, sugar and vanilla and beat until light and smooth. Then fold in the thickening lemon jelly and the yogurt. Spoon into the prepared tin and chill until set. Preheat the oven to 160°C/325°F/Gas 3.

Place two or three brandy snaps at a time on a baking sheet. Place in the oven for no longer than 1 minute, until soft enough to unroll and flatten out completely. Leave on a cold plate or tray to harden again. Repeat with the remaining brandy snaps.

To serve, turn the cheesecake out on to a board with the help of the clear film. Cut into eight slices and place one slice on each brandy snap base. Decorate with mint leaves and sprinkle with icing sugar.

COOK'S TIP
If you don't have any brandy snaps to hand, you could serve this cheesecake on thin slices of moist ginger cake, or on other thin, crisp biscuits.

APPLE AND HAZELNUT SHORTCAKE

This variation of a traditional recipe will be popular with all the family.

Serves 8–10

150g/5oz/1¼ cups wholemeal flour

50g/2oz/½ cup ground hazelnuts

90ml/6 tbsp icing sugar, sifted

*150g/5oz/generous ½ cup unsalted
   butter or margarine*

3 sharp eating apples

5ml/1 tsp lemon juice

*15–30ml/1–2 tbsp caster sugar, or to
   taste*

*15ml/1 tbsp chopped fresh mint, or
   5ml/1 tsp dried*

*250ml/8fl oz/1 cup whipping cream or
   crème fraîche*

few drops of vanilla essence

*few mint sprigs and whole hazelnuts,
   to decorate*

Process the flour, ground hazelnuts and icing sugar with the butter in a food processor or blender in short bursts, or rub the butter into the dry ingredients until they come together into a ball. (Don't overwork the mixture.) Add a very little iced water if necessary. Knead briefly, then chill, covered or wrapped, for about 30 minutes.

Preheat the oven to 160°C/325°F/Gas 3. Cut the chilled dough in half and roll out each half, on a lightly floured surface, to form an 18cm/7in round. Place on greaseproof paper on baking sheets and bake for about 40 minutes, or until crisp. If the shortcakes are browning too much, move them down in the oven to a lower shelf. Allow to cool.

Peel, core and chop the apples into a pan with the lemon juice. Add sugar to taste, then cook for about 2–3 minutes, until just softening. Mash the apple gently with the fresh mint or dried and leave to cool.

Whip the cream or crème fraîche with the vanilla essence. Place one shortcake base on a serving plate. Carefully spread half the apple and then half the cream or crème fraîche on top of the shortcake.

Place the second shortcake on top, then spread over the remaining apple and cream, swirling the top layer of cream gently. Serve immediately decorated with mint sprigs and a few whole hazelnuts.

LEMON MERINGUE PIE

A classic, popular pie with a piquant filling and golden meringue topping.

Serves 6–8

275g/10oz/1⅓ cups caster sugar

25g/1oz/¼ cup cornflour

pinch of salt

30ml/2 tbsp finely grated lemon rind

120ml/4fl oz/½ cup fresh lemon juice

250ml/8fl oz/1 cup water

3 eggs, separated

40g/1½oz/3 tbsp butter

23cm/9in pastry case

pinch of cream of tartar (if needed)

COOK'S TIP

Egg whites can be beaten to their greatest volume if they are at room temperature rather than cold. A copper bowl and wire balloon whisk are the best tools to use, although a stainless-steel bowl and electric mixer produce very good results. Take care not to over-beat whites (they will look grainy and separate).

Combine 200g/7oz/1 cup sugar, the cornflour, salt and lemon rind in a saucepan. Stir in the lemon juice and water until smoothly blended.

Bring to the boil over medium-high heat, stirring constantly. Simmer until the mixture is thickened, about 1 minute.

Blend in the egg yolks. Cook the mixture over medium-low heat for a further 2 minutes, stirring constantly.

Remove the saucepan from the heat. Add the butter and mix well.

Pour the lemon filling into the pastry case. Spread it evenly and level the surface with a palette knife. Leave to cool completely.

Preheat the oven to 180°C/350°F/Gas 4.

In a scrupulously clean, grease-free bowl, beat the egg whites until they will hold soft peaks. (If not using a copper bowl, add the cream of tartar as soon as the whites are frothy.) Add the remaining sugar and continue beating until the mixture is stiff and glossy.

Spread the meringue evenly over the filling with a palette knife. Take care to seal it to the edges of the pastry case all round.

Bake for 10–15 minutes or until the meringue is just set and lightly golden brown on the surface. Leave to cool before serving.

BOSTON BANOFFEE PIE

Guaranteed to bring a grin to diners' faces, this is a winning combination of bananas and toffee.

Makes a 20cm/8in pie

20cm/8in cooked pastry case, cooled

2 small bananas, sliced

a little lemon juice

whipped cream and grated plain chocolate, to decorate

For the filling

115g/4oz/½ cup butter

½ x 400g/14oz can sweetened condensed milk

115g/4oz/⅔ cup soft light brown sugar

30ml/2 tbsp golden syrup

COOK'S TIP

To make the pastry case, rub 115g/4oz/½ cup butter into 150g/5oz/1¼ cups plain flour. Stir in 60ml/4 tbsp caster sugar and press into a 20cm/8in flan tin. Fill with crumpled foil and bake at 160°C/325°F/Gas 3 for 20–25 minutes.

Make the filling. Place the butter, condensed milk, brown sugar and golden syrup in a large non-stick saucepan. Heat gently, stirring occasionally, until the sugar has dissolved.

Bring to a gentle boil and cook for 7 minutes, stirring all the time (to prevent burning), until the mixture thickens and turns a light caramel colour. Pour into the cooked pastry case and leave until cold.

Decorate with the bananas dipped in the lemon juice. Pipe a swirl of whipped cream in the centre and sprinkle with the grated chocolate.

SUMMER PUDDING

This is a classic English dessert, traditionally made in midsummer.

Serves 4

about 8 thin slices day-old white bread,
* crusts removed*
750g/1³/4lb/7 cups mixed berries
about 30ml/2 tbsp sugar

COOK'S TIP
Use a selection of soft, juicy
berries such as redcurrants,
raspberries and blackberries.

Cut a round from one slice of bread to fit in the base of a 1.2 litre/2 pint/ 5 cup pudding basin, then cut strips of bread about 5cm/2in wide to line the basin, overlapping the strips.

Gently heat the fruit, sugar and 30ml/2 tbsp water in a large heavy saucepan, shaking the pan occasionally, until the juices begin to run.

Reserve about 45ml/3 tbsp fruit juice, then spoon the fruit and remaining juice into the basin, taking care not to dislodge the bread.

Cut the remaining bread to fit entirely over the fruit. Stand the basin on a plate and cover with a saucer or small plate that will just fit inside the top of the basin. Place a heavy weight on top. Chill the pudding and the reserved fruit juice overnight. Run a knife around the inside of the basin, then invert the pudding on to a plate. Pour over the reserved juice and serve.

hot desserts

Apple pies will often first spring to mind at the mention
of hot fruit desserts, but bananas, pears, citrus fruits and
various berries are equally versatile and make a valuable
contribution to the repertoire of dishes. Simple and
speedy recipes include scrumptious Hot Bananas with
Rum and Raisins, glistening Red Berry Tart with Lemon
Cream Filling or extra special Apple Couscous Pudding.

SPICED NUTTY BANANAS

Baked bananas are delectable however you serve them, but with a triple nut topping they are delicious.

Serves 3

6 ripe, but firm, bananas
30ml/2 tbsp chopped, unsalted cashew nuts
30ml/2 tbsp chopped, unsalted peanuts
30ml/2 tbsp desiccated coconut
15ml/1 tbsp demerara sugar
5ml/1 tsp ground cinnamon
2.5ml/½ tsp freshly grated nutmeg
150ml/¼ pint/⅔ cup orange juice
60ml/4 tbsp rum
15g/½oz/1 tbsp butter or margarine
double cream or Greek-style yogurt, to serve

Preheat the oven to 200°C/400°F/Gas 6. Slice the bananas and place in a large, greased, shallow ovenproof dish. Do not leave for long at this stage as the bananas will discolour.

Mix the cashew nuts, peanuts, coconut, sugar, cinnamon and nutmeg in a small bowl. Pour the orange juice and rum over the bananas, then sprinkle evenly with the nut and sugar mixture.

Dot the top evenly with butter or margarine. Bake for 15–20 minutes or until the bananas are golden brown and the sauce is bubbling.

Serve the bananas hot, with double cream or Greek-style yogurt.

COOK'S TIP

Freshly grated nutmeg makes all the difference to this dish. You can add more rum, if you like, and chopped mixed nuts can be used instead of unsalted peanuts.

KUMQUAT AND HONEY COMPOTE

Sun-ripened, warm and spicy ingredients, sweetened with honey, make the perfect winter dessert.

Serves 4

350g/12oz/2 cups kumquats

275g/10oz/1¼ cups dried apricots

30ml/2 tbsp raisins

30ml/2 tbsp lemon juice

1 orange

2.5cm/1in piece of fresh root ginger

4 cardamom pods

4 cloves

30ml/2 tbsp clear honey

15ml/1 tbsp flaked almonds, toasted,
to decorate

Wash the kumquats, and, if they are large, cut them in half. Place them in a large saucepan with the dried apricots and raisins. Pour over 300ml/½ pint/1¼ cups water and add the lemon juice. Bring to the boil.

Pare the rind thinly from the orange and add to the pan. Peel the ginger, grate it finely and add it to the pan. Lightly crush the cardamom pods and add them to the pan, with the cloves.

Lower the heat, cover the pan and simmer gently for about 30 minutes or until the fruit is tender, stirring occasionally.

Squeeze the juice from the orange and add it to the pan with the honey. Stir well, then taste and add more honey if required. Sprinkle with flaked almonds and serve warm.

VARIATION

If you prefer, use ready-to-eat dried apricots. Reduce the liquid to 300ml/½pint/1¼cups, and add the apricots for the last 5 minutes of cooking.

BANANA MANDAZIS

These delicious banana fritters come from Africa, where they are very popular.

Serves 4

1 egg

2 ripe bananas, roughly chopped

150ml/¼ pint/⅔ cup milk

2.5ml/½ tsp vanilla essence

225g/8oz/2 cups self-raising flour

5ml/1 tsp baking powder

45ml/3 tbsp granulated sugar

vegetable oil, for deep-frying

icing sugar, for dusting

COOK'S TIP

Drain each batch of mandazis well on kitchen paper and keep them hot in a low oven while you are cooking the remainder.

Place the egg, bananas, milk, vanilla essence, flour, baking powder and sugar in a blender or food processor. Process to a smooth, creamy batter. If it is too thick, add a little extra milk. Set aside for 10 minutes.

Heat the oil in a heavy-based saucepan or deep-fat fryer. When hot, carefully place spoonfuls of the mixture in the oil and fry for 3–4 minutes until golden. Remove with a slotted spoon and drain well. Keep hot while cooking the remaining mandazis. Dust with icing sugar and serve at once.

HOT BANANAS WITH RUM AND RAISINS

Choose almost-ripe bananas with evenly coloured skins, either all yellow or just green only at the tips.
Black patches indicate that the fruit is over-ripe.

Serves 4

40g/1½oz/¼ cup seedless raisins

75ml/5 tbsp dark rum

50g/2oz/4 tbsp unsalted butter

60ml/4 tbsp soft light brown sugar

4 ripe bananas, peeled and
*   halved lengthways*

1.5ml/¼ tsp grated nutmeg

1.5ml/¼ tsp ground cinnamon

30ml/2 tbsp slivered almonds, toasted

chilled cream or vanilla ice cream, to
*   serve (optional)*

Put the raisins in a bowl and pour over the rum. Leave to soak for about 30 minutes, by which time the raisins will have plumped up.

Melt the butter in a frying pan, add the brown sugar and stir until just dissolved. Add the bananas and cook them for 4–5 minutes until they are just tender.

Sprinkle the nutmeg and cinnamon over the bananas, then pour over the rum and raisins. Stand back and carefully set the rum alight, using a long taper, and stir gently to mix.

Scatter the slivered almonds over the bananas and serve immediately with chilled cream or vanilla ice cream, if you like. Crème fraîche or Greek-style yogurt would also make a delicious accompaniment for the bananas.

VARIATION
Use sultanas soaked in a tangerine-flavoured liqueur, such as Van der Hum, or an orange-flavoured liqueur, such as Grand Marnier, instead of raisins in rum.

BAKED APPLES WITH CARAMEL SAUCE

The creamy caramel sauce adds a touch of sophistication to this traditional dish.

Serves 6

3 Granny Smith apples, cored but
not peeled
3 Red Delicious apples, cored but
not peeled
150g/5oz/³⁄₄ cup soft brown sugar
175ml/6fl oz/³⁄₄ cup water
2.5ml/¹⁄₂ tsp grated nutmeg
1.5ml/¹⁄₄ tsp ground
black pepper
40g/1¹⁄₂oz/¹⁄₄ cup walnut pieces
40g/1¹⁄₂oz/¹⁄₄ cup sultanas
50g/2oz/4 tbsp butter or
margarine, diced

For the caramel sauce
15g/¹⁄₂ oz/1 tbsp butter or margarine
120ml/4fl oz/¹⁄₂ cup whipping cream

COOK'S TIP
Use a mixture of firm red and
gold pears instead of the apples.
Cook for 10 minutes longer.

Preheat the oven to 190°C/375°F/Gas 5. Lightly grease a baking tin. With a small knife, enlarge the core opening at the stem end of each apple to about 2.5cm/1in in diameter. Arrange the apples in the tin, stem-end up.

In a small pan, combine the brown sugar, water, nutmeg and pepper. Boil the mixture, stirring, for 6 minutes. Mix together the walnuts and sultanas. Spoon some of the walnut mixture into each apple. Top with some diced butter or margarine. Spoon the sugar sauce over and around the apples. Bake, basting occasionally, until the apples are just tender, about 50 minutes. Put the apples in a serving dish, reserving the sauce in the baking dish. Keep the apples warm.

To make the caramel sauce, mix the butter or margarine, cream and reserved sauce in a pan. Bring to the boil, stirring, and simmer for 2 minutes until thickened. Let the sauce cool slightly before serving.

CARAMELIZED APPLES

A sweet, sticky dessert which is very quickly made, and usually very quickly eaten!

Serves 4

675g/1½lb eating apples
115g/4oz/½ cup unsalted butter
25g/1oz/7 tbsp fresh white
*   breadcrumbs*
50g/2oz/½ cup ground almonds
finely grated rind of 2 lemons
60ml/4 tbsp golden syrup
60ml/4 tbsp clotted cream, to serve

COOK'S TIP

The easiest and quickest way to make breadcrumbs is to put slices of bread into a food processor or blender. Roughly chop the bread for several seconds until breadcrumbs form. Take care not to overchop.

Peel and core the apples. Cut them into 1cm/½in thick rings. Heat a wok and add the butter. When the butter has melted, add the apple rings and stir-fry for 4 minutes until golden and tender. Remove from the wok, reserving the butter. Add the breadcrumbs to the hot butter and stir-fry for 1 minute.

Stir in the ground almonds and lemon rind and stir-fry for a further 3 minutes, stirring constantly. Sprinkle the breadcrumb mix over the apples, then drizzle warmed golden syrup over the top. Serve with the cream.

CHOCOLATE CHIP BANANA PANCAKES

Serve these delicious banana pancakes as a dessert topped with cream and toasted almonds.

Makes 16

2 ripe bananas

200ml/7fl oz/scant 1 cup milk

2 eggs

150g/5oz/1¼ cups self-raising flour

25g/1oz/⅓ cup ground almonds

15ml/1 tbsp caster sugar

25g/1oz/3 tbsp plain chocolate chips

butter, for frying

pinch of salt

For the topping

150ml/¼ pint/⅔ cup double cream

15ml/1 tbsp icing sugar

50g/2oz/½ cup toasted flaked almonds

VARIATION

For banana and blueberry pancakes, replace the chocolate chips with 115g/4oz/1 cup fresh blueberries. Hot pancakes are simply delicious served with ice cream.

In a bowl, mash the bananas with a fork. Mix in half of the milk, then beat in the eggs. Sift in the flour and add the ground almonds, sugar and salt. Mix lightly. Add the remaining milk and stir in the chocolate chips to produce a thick batter.

Heat a knob of butter in a large, non-stick frying pan. Spoon the pancake mixture into heaps, allowing room for them to spread. When bubbles appear on top of the pancakes, turn them over and cook briefly on the other side. Remove and keep hot.

Whip the cream lightly with the icing sugar. Spoon on to the pancakes and top each with a few flaked almonds.

BANANA, MAPLE AND LIME PANCAKES

Pancakes are a treat any day of the week, especially when they are filled with bananas and maple syrup.

Serves 4

115g/4oz/1 cup plain flour

1 egg white

250ml/8fl oz/1 cup milk

sunflower oil, for frying

strips of lime rind, to decorate

For the filling

4 bananas, sliced

45ml/3 tbsp maple syrup or
*   golden syrup*

30ml/2 tbsp fresh lime juice

COOK'S TIP

Pancakes freeze well. To store for later use, stack and interleave them with non-stick baking paper, overwrap with foil and freeze for up to 3 months. Thaw thoroughly and reheat before using.

Mix the flour, egg white and milk in a bowl. Add 60ml/4 tbsp cold water and whisk until smooth and bubbly. Chill until needed.

Heat a little oil in a non-stick frying pan and swirl in enough batter just to coat the base. Cook until golden, then turn over and cook the other side. Keep hot while making the remaining pancakes.

Make the filling. Place the bananas, syrup and lime juice in a pan and simmer gently for 1 minute. Spoon into the pancakes and fold into quarters. Sprinkle with strips of lime rind to decorate.

LEMON PANCAKES

Thin, lacy pancakes, or crêpes, are wonderfully versatile. They are good served very simply with just lemon juice and sugar.

Makes about 12

170g/6oz/1 cup plain flour

10ml/2 tsp caster sugar (for sweet pancakes)

2 eggs

450ml/³/4 pint/1⁷/8 cups milk

about 30g/1oz/2 tbsp melted butter

lemon juice, to serve

sugar, to serve (optional)

PANCAKE-MAKING TIPS

● *Pancake batter should be the consistency of whipping cream. If the batter is at all lumpy, strain it. If it doesn't flow smoothly to make a thin pancake, add more liquid.*

● *Pancake batter can be made in either a blender or food processor. It must have time to stand before using, to incorporate more air.*

To make the pancake batter, mix together the flour, sugar (for sweet pancakes), eggs and milk. Leave to stand for 20 minutes. Heat a 20cm/8in pancake pan over a moderate heat. The pan is ready when a few drops of water sprinkled on the surface jump and sizzle immediately. Grease the pan lightly with a little melted butter. Pour 45–60ml/3–4 tbsp batter into the pan. Quickly tilt and rotate the pan so the batter spreads out to cover the bottom thinly and evenly; pour out any excess batter.

Cook for 30–45 seconds or until the pancake is set and small holes have appeared. If the cooking seems to be taking too long, increase the heat slightly. Lift the edge of the pancake with a palette knife; the base of the pancake should be lightly brown. Shake the pan vigorously back and forth to loosen the pancake completely, then turn or flip it over. Cook the other side for about 30 seconds. Serve sprinkled with lemon juice and sugar, if using.

APPLE SOUFFLE OMELETTE

Apples sautéed until they are slightly caramelized make a delicious autumn filling for omelettes.

Serves 2

4 eggs, separated
30ml/2 tbsp single cream
15ml/1 tbsp caster sugar
15g/¹/₂oz/1 tbsp butter
icing sugar, for dredging

For the filling

25g/1oz/2 tbsp butter
30ml/2 tbsp soft light brown sugar
1 eating apple, peeled, cored and sliced
45ml/3 tbsp single cream

To make the filling, heat the butter and sugar in a frying pan and sauté the apple slices until just tender. Stir in the cream and keep warm.

Place the egg yolks in a bowl with the cream and sugar and beat well. Whisk the egg whites until stiff, then fold into the yolk mixture.

Melt the butter in a large heavy-based frying pan, pour in the soufflé mixture and spread evenly. Cook for 1 minute until golden underneath, then place under a hot grill to brown the top.

Slide the omelette on to a plate, add the apple mixture, then fold over. Sift the icing sugar over thickly, then mark in a criss-cross pattern with a hot metal skewer. Serve immediately.

STRAWBERRY AND APPLE TART

A dish for lovers – apples and strawberries in perfect harmony.

Serves 4–6

*2 tart Bramley cooking apples (about
    450g/1lb), peeled, cored and sliced
200g/7oz/1¾ cups strawberries,
    halved
60ml/4 tbsp sugar
15ml/1 tbsp cornflour*

*For the pastry
150g/5oz/1¼ cups self-raising flour
50g/2oz/⅔ cup rolled oats
50g/2oz/4 tbsp margarine*

COOK'S TIP

*It is best to prepare apples just
before you use them. If you do
prepare them ahead, place the
cut pieces in a bowl of lemony
cold water to prevent them from
turning brown.*

Preheat the oven to 200°C/400°F/Gas 6. For the pastry, mix the flour and oats in a bowl and rub in the margarine evenly. Stir in cold water to bind and form a ball. Knead lightly until smooth. On a lightly floured surface, roll out the pastry and line a lightly greased 23cm/9in loose-based flan tin. Trim the edges, prick the base, line the pastry with greaseproof paper and fill with baking beans. Roll out the trimmings and make heart shapes with a cutter. Bake for 10 minutes, remove the paper and beans, and bake for 10–15 minutes until golden brown. Bake the hearts until golden. Place the apples in a pan with the strawberries, sugar and cornflour. Cover and cook gently, stirring, until the fruit is just tender. Spoon into the pastry case and decorate with the pastry hearts.

APPLE MERINGUE TART

Like pears, quinces substitute well in most apple recipes and are quite delicious. If you ever find any quinces, this is the ideal tart to use them in.

Serves 6
675g/1½lb eating apples
juice of ½ lemon
25g/1oz/2 tbsp butter
60ml/4 tbsp demerara sugar
cream, to serve (optional)

For the pastry
50g/2oz/½ cup plain flour
75g/3oz/¾ cup wholemeal flour
pinch of salt
115g/4oz/½ cup caster sugar
75g/3oz/6 tbsp butter
1 egg, separated, plus 1 egg white

To make the pastry, sift the flours into a bowl with the salt, adding in the wheat flakes from the sieve. Add 15ml/1 tbsp of the caster sugar and rub in the butter until the mixture forms soft crumbs.

Work in the egg yolk and, if necessary, 15–30ml/1–2 tbsp cold water. Knead lightly and bring together into a ball. Chill, covered or wrapped, for between 10 and 20 minutes.

Preheat the oven to 190°C/375°F/Gas 5. Roll the chilled pastry out on a lightly floured surface to form a 23cm/9in round and use to line a 20cm/8in flan tin. Line with greaseproof paper and fill with baking beans. Bake blind for 15 minutes, then remove the paper and beans and cook for a further 5–10 minutes, until the pastry is crisp.

Meanwhile, peel, core and slice the apples, then toss in lemon juice. Melt the butter, add the demerara sugar and fry the apple until golden and just tender. Arrange in the pastry case.

Preheat the oven to 220°C/425°F/Gas 7. Whisk the egg white until it is stiff. Whisk in half the remaining caster sugar, then carefully fold in the rest. Pipe the meringue over the apples. Bake for 6–7 minutes. Serve the tart hot or cold, with cream if wished.

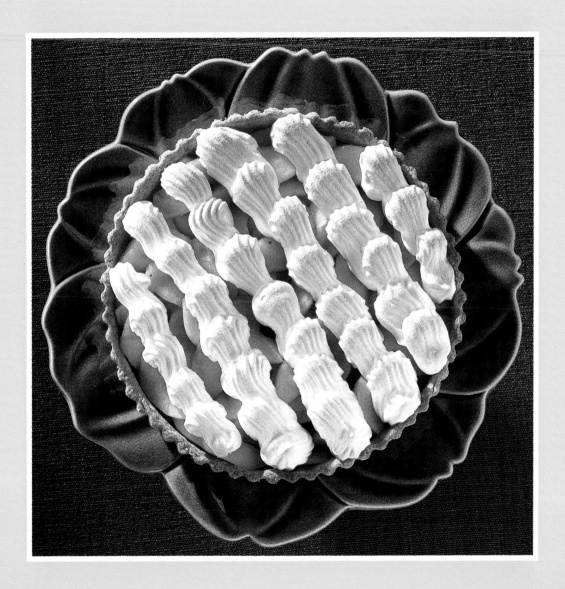

DUTCH APPLE TART

Flaked almonds give this tart a wonderful crunchiness.

Serves 4–6

*6 eating apples, peeled, cored
 and grated*
60ml/4 tbsp soft light brown sugar
1.5ml/¼ tsp vanilla essence
2.5ml/¼ tsp ground cinnamon
25g/1oz/scant ¼ cup raisins
25g/1oz/¼ cup flaked almonds, toasted
15ml/1 tbsp caster sugar, for dredging
whipped cream, to serve

For the pastry

175g/6oz/1½ cups plain flour
*130g/4½oz/generous ½ cup butter,
 cubed and softened*
90ml/6 tbsp caster sugar
pinch of salt

Preheat the oven to 180°C/350°F/Gas 4. Lightly butter a 20cm/8in round springform tin and dust with a little plain flour.

To make the pastry, place the flour in a mixing bowl with the butter and sugar, then squeeze together to form a firm dough. Knead the pastry lightly and bring it together into a ball. Chill, covered or wrapped, for 1 hour.

Roll two-thirds of the chilled pastry out on a lightly floured surface to form a 25cm/10in round. Use this to line the base and two-thirds up the sides of the prepared tin, pressing the pastry up the sides with your fingers. Trim away any excess pastry.

Mix together the apples, sugar, vanilla essence, cinnamon, raisins and almonds in a bowl. Spoon into the lined tin and level the surface. Fold the pastry edge above the level of the apples down over the filling.

Roll out the remaining pastry and cut into eight 1cm/½in strips. Brush the strips with cold water and sprinkle over the caster sugar. Lay the strips on top of the tart in a lattice pattern, securing the ends to the folded-over edge with a little water.

Bake in the centre of the oven for 1 hour, or until the pastry is golden brown. Remove and leave to cool in the tin. When the tart is cold, carefully remove it from the tin. Serve cut into slices with whipped cream.

RED BERRY SPONGE TART

Use a selection of berries for this delicious sponge tart. Serve warm from the oven with vanilla ice cream.

Serves 4

softened butter, for greasing
450g/1lb/3 cups soft berry fruits, such
*   as raspberries, blackberries,*
*   blackcurrants, redcurrants,*
*   strawberries or blueberries*
2 eggs, at room temperature
50g/2oz/¼ cup caster sugar, plus extra
*   to taste (optional)*
15ml/1 tbsp plain flour
50g/2oz/¾ cup ground almonds
vanilla ice cream, to serve

VARIATION

When berry fruits are out of
season, use thawed frozen fruits,
or alternatively use bottled
fruits, but ensure that they are
well drained before use.

Preheat the oven to 190°C/375°F/Gas 5. Brush the base and sides of a 23cm/9in flan tin with softened butter and line the base with a circle of non-stick baking paper. Scatter the fruits in the tin with a little sugar, to taste, if the fruits are tart.

Whisk the eggs and sugar together for about 3–4 minutes or until they leave a thick trail across the surface. Combine the flour and almonds, then fold into the egg mixture with a spatula – retaining as much air as possible.

Spread the mixture on top of the fruit base and bake in the oven for 15 minutes. Transfer to a serving plate and serve with vanilla ice cream.

LEMON ALMOND TART

This classic tart is fresh-tasting, with a crisp, sweet pastry case.

Serves 8

225g/8oz shortcrust pastry
75g/3oz/³⁄₄ cup blanched almonds
115g/4oz/¹⁄₂ cup sugar
2 eggs
grated rind and juice of 1¹⁄₂ lemons
115g/4oz/¹⁄₂ cup butter, melted
strips of lemon rind, to decorate

Roll out the pastry to about 3mm/⅛in thick and transfer to a 23cm/9in pie tin. Trim the edge. Prick the base all over with a fork and chill for at least 20 minutes. Preheat the oven to 200°C/400°F/Gas 6. Line the tart base with crumpled greaseproof paper and fill with pie weights. Bake for 12 minutes. Remove the paper and weights and continue baking until golden, about 6–8 minutes. Reduce the oven temperature to 180°C/350°F/Gas 4. Grind the almonds finely with 15ml/1 tbsp of the sugar in a food processor, blender, or grinder. Set a mixing bowl over a pan of hot water. Add the eggs and the remaining sugar, and beat until the mixture is very thick. Stir in the lemon rind and juice, butter, and ground almonds.

Pour into the pastry case. Bake until the filling is golden and set, for about 35 minutes. Decorate with lemon rind.

RED BERRY TART WITH LEMON CREAM FILLING

Just right for warm summer days, this flan is best filled just before serving so the pastry remains mouth-wateringly crisp. Select red berries such as strawberries, raspberries or redcurrants.

Serves 6–8
150g/5oz/1¼ cups plain flour
25g/1oz/¼ cup cornflour
30g/1½oz/3 tbsp icing sugar
100g/3½oz/8 tbsp butter
5ml/1 tsp vanilla essence
2 egg yolks, beaten

For the filling
200g/7oz/scant 1 cup cream
  cheese, softened
45ml/3 tbsp lemon curd
grated rind and juice of 1 lemon
icing sugar, to sweeten (optional)
225g/8oz/1½ cups mixed red
  berry fruits
45ml/3 tbsp redcurrant jelly

Sift the flour, cornflour and icing sugar together, then rub in the butter until the mixture resembles breadcrumbs.

Beat the vanilla into the egg yolks, then mix into the crumbs to make a firm dough, adding cold water if necessary.

Roll out and line a 23cm/9in round flan tin, pressing the dough well up the sides after trimming. Prick the base of the flan with a fork and leave to rest in the fridge for 30 minutes.

Preheat the oven to 200°C/400°F/Gas 6. Line the flan with greaseproof paper and baking beans. Place the tin on a baking sheet and bake for 20 minutes, removing the paper and beans for the last 5 minutes. When cooked, cool and remove the pastry case from the flan tin.

Cream the cheese, lemon curd and lemon rind and juice, adding icing sugar to sweeten, if you wish. Spread the mixture into the base of the flan.

Top the flan with the fruits. Warm the redcurrant jelly and trickle it over the fruits just before serving.

VARIATION
Leave out the redcurrant jelly and sprinkle with icing sugar.

TARTE TATIN

This delicious caramelized fruit tart from France was originally created by the Tatin sisters who ran a popular restaurant in Sologne in the Orléanais.

Serves 4

75g/3oz/6 tbsp butter, softened
90ml/6 tbsp soft light brown sugar
10 Cox's Pippin, peeled, cored and
  thickly sliced
whipped cream, to serve (optional)

For the pastry

50g/2oz/4 tbsp butter, softened
45ml/3 tbsp caster sugar
1 egg
115g/4oz/1 cup plain flour
pinch of salt

> COOK'S TIP
> Cox's Pippins apples are perfect
> for this tart because they hold
> their shape so well. If they are
> not available, use another firm,
> sweet eating apple instead.

To make the pastry, cream the butter and sugar in a bowl until pale and creamy. Beat in the egg, then sift in the flour and salt and mix to a soft dough. On a lightly floured surface, knead gently and bring the dough together into a ball.

Grease a 23cm/9in cake tin, then add 50g/2oz/4 tbsp of the butter. Place the cake tin on the hob and melt the butter gently. Remove from the heat and sprinkle over 60ml/4 tbsp of the sugar.

Arrange the apple slices on top, then sprinkle with the remaining sugar and dot with the remaining butter.

Preheat the oven to 230°C/450°F/Gas 8. Place the cake tin on the hob again over a low to moderate heat for about 15 minutes, until a light golden caramel forms on the base. Remove the tin from the heat.

Roll out the pastry on a lightly floured surface to a round the same size as the tin and lay on top of the apples. Tuck the pastry edges down round the sides of the apples. Trim away any excess pastry.

Bake for about 20–25 minutes, until the pastry is golden brown. Remove the tart from the oven and leave to stand for about 5 minutes.

Place an upturned plate on top of the tin and, holding the two together with a dish towel, turn the apple tart out on to the plate. Serve while still warm with whipped cream, if wished.

STRAWBERRY AND BLUEBERRY PIE

This tart works equally well using any combination of berries that are available, as long as there is a riot of colour and the fruit is in perfect condition.

Serves 6–8
225g/8oz/2 cups plain flour
pinch of salt
75g/3oz/9 tbsp icing sugar
150g/5oz/10 tbsp unsalted butter, diced
1 egg yolk

For the filling
350g/12oz/1¼ cups mascarpone cheese
30ml/2 tbsp icing sugar
few drops vanilla essence
finely grated rind of 1 orange
450–675g/1–1½lb/3–5 cups fresh
  mixed strawberries and blueberries
90ml/6 tbsp redcurrant jelly
30ml/2 tbsp orange juice

Sift the flour, salt and sugar into a bowl, and rub in the butter until the mixture resembles coarse crumbs. Using a round-bladed knife, mix in the egg yolk and 10ml/2 tsp cold water. Gather the dough together, then turn out on to a floured surface and knead lightly until smooth. Wrap in clear film and chill in the fridge for 1 hour.

Preheat the oven to 190°C/375°F/Gas 5. Roll out the pastry and use to line a 25cm/10in fluted flan tin. Prick the base and chill for 15 minutes.

Line the chilled pastry case with greaseproof paper and baking beans, then bake for 15 minutes. Remove the paper and beans and bake for a further 15 minutes, until crisp and golden. Leave to cool in the tin.

Beat together the mascarpone, sugar, vanilla essence and orange rind in a mixing bowl until the mixture is smooth.

Remove the pastry case from the tin, then spoon in the filling and pile the fruits on top. Heat the redcurrant jelly with the orange juice until runny, sieve if necessary, then brush over the fruit to glaze.

APPLE PIE

A comforting dish that will take you back to your childhood.

Serves 8

4 tart Granny Smith apples (about
  900g/2lb), sliced
15ml/1 tbsp fresh lemon juice
15ml/1 tbsp vanilla essence
115g/4oz/1/2 cup sugar
2.5ml/1/2 tsp ground cinnamon
20g/3/4oz/11/2 tbsp butter or margarine
1 egg yolk
10ml/2 tsp whipping cream

For the pastry

225g/8oz/2 cups self-raising flour
5ml/1 tsp salt
175g/6oz/3/4 cup lard
60–75ml/4–5 tbsp water
15ml/1 tbsp quick-cook tapioca

Preheat the oven to 230°C/450°F/Gas 8. To make the pastry, sift the flour and salt into a bowl. Rub in the lard until the mixture forms soft crumbs. Add the water, a tablespoon at a time, and form into a ball.

Cut the dough in half and shape each half into another ball. On a lightly floured surface, roll out one of the balls of pastry to a circle about 30cm/12in in diameter.

Line a lightly greased 23cm/9in loose-based flan tin, easing the dough in and being careful not to stretch it. Trim the edges carefully and keep the excess pastry for later. Sprinkle the quick-cook tapioca evenly over the base of the pastry case.

Roll out the remaining pastry to 3mm/1/8in thick and cut out eight large leaf shapes with a sharp knife. Cut the trimmings into enough smaller leaves to decorate the edges of the pie. Score the leaves with the back of a knife to make the leaf veins.

To make the filling, mix together the apples, lemon juice, vanilla essence, sugar and cinnamon. Tip into the pastry case and add dots of butter or margarine over the apple mixture.

Arrange the large pastry leaves in a decorative pattern on top, and decorate the edge with the smaller leaves. Mix the egg yolk with the cream and brush it over the leaves.

Bake in the preheated oven for 10 minutes. Reduce the oven temperature to 180°C/350°F/Gas 4. Cook for a further 35–45 minutes until the pastry is golden brown. Allow the pie to cool in the tin slightly before removing it and putting it on a wire cooling rack.

BLUEBERRY AND PEAR PIE

The combination of blueberries and pears makes a sweet and juicy pie. Serve warm with crème fraîche or try a scoop or two of vanilla ice cream.

Serves 4
225g/8oz/2 cups plain flour
pinch of salt
50g/2oz/4 tbsp lard, cubed
50g/2oz/4 tbsp butter, cubed
675g/1½lb/6 cups blueberries
30ml/2 tbsp caster sugar
15ml/1 tbsp arrowroot
2 ripe, but firm pears, peeled, cored and sliced
2.5ml/½ tsp ground cinnamon
grated rind of ½ lemon
beaten egg, to glaze
caster sugar, for sprinkling
crème fraîche, to serve

Sift the flour and salt into a bowl and rub in the lard and butter until the mixture resembles fine breadcrumbs. Stir in 45ml/3 tbsp cold water and mix to a dough. Chill for 30 minutes.

Place 225g/8oz/2 cups of the blueberries in a pan with the sugar. Cover and cook gently until the berries are soft. Press through a nylon sieve.

Blend the arrowroot with 30ml/2 tbsp cold water and add to the blueberry purée. Bring to the boil, stirring until thickened. Cool slightly.

Place a baking sheet in the oven and preheat to 190°C/375°F/Gas 5. Roll out just over half the pastry on a lightly floured surface and use to line a 20cm/8in shallow pie dish or plate.

Mix together the remaining blueberries, the pears, cinnamon and lemon rind and spoon into the dish. Pour over the blueberry purée.

Roll out the remaining pastry and use to cover the pie. Make a small slit in the centre. Brush with egg and sprinkle with sugar. Bake on the hot baking sheet, for 40–45 minutes, until golden. Serve warm with crème fraîche.

APPLE AND PEAR FRYING PAN CAKE

This unusual cake, lightly spiced with cinnamon and nutmeg and baked in a frying pan, is impressively simple to make. It is delicious served hot.

Serves 6

1 cooking apple (about 225g/8oz), peeled, cored and thinly sliced

1 pear, peeled, cored and thinly sliced

50g/2oz/¹/₂ cup chopped walnuts

5ml/1 tsp ground cinnamon

5ml/1 tsp grated nutmeg

3 eggs

75g/3oz/³/₄ cup plain flour

30ml/2 tbsp light brown sugar

175ml/6fl oz/³/₄ cup milk

5ml/1 tsp vanilla essence

50g/2 oz/4 tbsp butter or margarine

icing sugar, for sprinkling

cream or ice cream, to serve (optional)

Preheat the oven to 190°C/375°F/Gas 5. In a large bowl, toss together the apple and pear slices, walnuts, cinnamon and nutmeg until thoroughly combined. Set aside.

With an electric mixer, beat together the eggs, plain flour, light brown sugar, milk and vanilla essence. Melt the butter or margarine in a 23–25cm/9–10in ovenproof frying pan over moderate heat. Add the apple mixture and cook for about 5 minutes, until it is lightly caramelized, stirring occasionally. When cooked, make sure that the apple and pear mixture is evenly distributed in the frying pan.

Pour the sponge mixture over the fruit and nuts. Transfer the frying pan to the preheated oven and bake for about 30 minutes until the cake is puffy and pulling away from the sides of the pan. Serve hot sprinkled lightly with icing sugar, with cream or ice cream as an accompaniment, if you wish.

COOK'S TIP

This cake should be served straight from the frying pan. There is no need to transfer it to a serving plate first.

APPLE AND BLACKBERRY NUT CRUMBLE

This much-loved dish is perhaps one of the simplest and most delicious of hot British puddings.

Serves 4

4 Bramley cooking apples (about 900g/
   2lb), peeled, cored and sliced
115g/4oz/1/2 cup butter, cubed
115g/4oz/generous 1/2 cup soft light
   brown sugar
175g/6oz/13/4 cups blackberries

For the topping
75g/3oz/1/4 cup wholemeal flour
75g/3oz/1/4 cup plain flour
2.5ml/1/2 tsp ground cinnamon
45ml/3 tbsp chopped mixed
   nuts, toasted
custard, cream or ice cream, to serve

Preheat the oven to 180°C/350°F/Gas 4. Lightly butter a 1.2 litre/2 pint/ 5 cup ovenproof dish.

Place the apples in a pan with 25g/1oz/2 tbsp of the butter, 30ml/2 tbsp of the sugar and 15ml/1 tbsp water. Cover and cook gently for 10 minutes, until just tender. Remove from the heat and gently stir in the blackberries. Spoon the mixture into the dish and set aside.

To make the topping, sift the flours and cinnamon into a bowl (tip in any wheat flakes left in the sieve). Add the remaining butter and rub into the flour with your fingertips until the mixture resembles fine breadcrumbs.

Stir in the remaining 90ml/6 tbsp sugar and the nuts and mix well. Sprinkle the crumble topping over the fruit. Bake for 35–40 minutes, until the top is golden brown. Serve hot with custard, cream or ice cream.

APPLE COUSCOUS PUDDING

This unusual couscous mixture makes a delicious pudding with a rich fruity flavour, but virtually no fat.

Serves 4

600ml/1 pint/2½ cups apple juice

115g/4oz/⅔ cup couscous

40g/1½oz/¼ cup sultanas

2.5ml/½ tsp mixed spice

*1 large Bramley cooking apple (about
  225g/8oz), peeled, cored and sliced*

30ml/2 tbsp demerara sugar

natural low-fat yogurt, to serve

Preheat the oven to 200°C/400°F/Gas 6. Place the apple juice, couscous, sultanas and spice in a pan and bring to the boil, stirring. Cover and simmer for 10–12 minutes, until all the free liquid is absorbed.

Spoon half the couscous mixture into a 1.2 litre/2 pint/5 cup ovenproof dish and top with half the apple slices. Top with the remaining couscous.

Arrange the remaining apple slices overlapping over the top and sprinkle with demerara sugar. Bake in the oven for 25–30 minutes, or until golden brown. Serve hot with yogurt.

COOK'S TIP

*To ring the changes, substitute
other dried fruits for the sultanas
in this recipe – try chopped dates
or ready-to-eat pears, figs,
peaches or apricots.*

APPLE AND KUMQUAT SPONGE PUDDINGS

The kumquats provide a surprising tanginess in this pudding.

Serves 8

*150g/5oz/generous ½ cup butter, at
    room temperature*

*175g/6oz cooking apples, peeled and
    thinly sliced*

75g/3oz kumquats, thinly sliced

*150g/5oz/generous ½ cup golden
    caster sugar*

2 eggs

115g/4oz/1 cup self-raising flour

For the sauce

75g/3oz kumquats, thinly sliced

90ml/6 tbsp caster sugar

250ml/8fl oz/1 cup water

150ml/¼ pint/⅔ cup crème fraîche

*5ml/1 tsp cornflour mixed with 10ml/
    2 tsp water*

lemon juice, to taste

Prepare the steamer. Lightly butter eight 150ml/¼ pint/⅔ cup dariole moulds or ramekins and put a disc of buttered greaseproof paper on the base of each one.

Melt 25g/1oz/2 tbsp butter in a frying pan. Add the apples, kumquats and 30ml/2 tbsp sugar and cook over a moderate heat for 5–8 minutes or until the apples start to soften and the sugar begins to caramelize. Remove from the heat and leave to cool.

Meanwhile, cream the remaining butter with the remaining sugar until the mixture is pale and fluffy. Add the eggs, one at a time, beating well after each addition. Fold in the flour.

Divide the apple and kumquat mixture among the prepared moulds. Top with the sponge mixture. Cover the moulds and put them into the steamer. Steam on top of the stove for 45 minutes.

To make the sauce, put the kumquats, sugar and water in a frying pan and bring to the boil, stirring to dissolve the sugar. Simmer for 5 minutes. Stir in the crème fraîche and bring back to the boil, stirring.

Remove from the heat and whisk in the cornflour mixture. Return the pan to the heat and simmer gently for a further 2 minutes, stirring. Add lemon juice to taste. Turn out the puddings and serve hot with the sauce.

cakes and tea breads

Everyone is familiar with the use of dried fruit in cakes
and tea breads, but the following recipes show what
fabulous results can be achieved with fresh fruit.
Some of the cakes and breads may be enjoyed either
warm from the oven or at room temperature.
Try Apple Crumble Cake, Orange Honey Bread,
Warm Lemon and Syrup Cake or the luscious
Chocolate Cake with Banana Sauce.

LEMON COCONUT LAYER CAKE

This delightful layered cake has a tangy lemon custard filling and a light lemony icing, contrasting with the crunchy coconut topping.

Serves 8–10

115g/4oz/1 cup flour

pinch of salt

8 eggs

350g/12oz/1¾ cups granulated sugar

15ml/1 tbsp grated orange rind

grated rind of 2 lemons

juice of 1 lemon

40g/1½oz/½ cup shredded coconut

30ml/2 tbsp cornflour

250ml/8fl oz/1 cup water

75g/3oz/6 tbsp butter

For the icing

115g/4oz/½ cup unsalted butter, at
     room temperature

150g/5oz/1 cup icing sugar

grated rind of 1 lemon

90ml/6 tbsp fresh lemon juice, plus
     more if needed

400g/14oz shredded coconut

Preheat the oven to 180°C/350°F/Gas 4. Line three 20cm/8in round cake tins with greaseproof paper and grease. In a large bowl, sift together the flour and salt and set aside.

Place six of the eggs in a large heatproof bowl set over hot water. With an electric mixer, beat until frothy. Gradually beat in 150g/5oz/¾ cup of the sugar until the mixture doubles in volume, for about 10 minutes.

Remove the bowl from the hot water. Fold in the orange rind and half of the grated lemon rind. Gently stir in 15ml/1 tbsp of the lemon juice. Fold in the coconut. Sift over the flour mixture in three batches, folding in after each addition. Divide the mixture among the prepared tins.

Bake until the cakes pull away from the sides of the tin, 25–30 minutes. Leave to stand for 3–5 minutes, then unmould and transfer to a wire rack.

In a bowl, blend the cornflour with a little cold water to dissolve. Whisk in the remaining eggs just until blended. Set aside.

In a saucepan, combine the remaining lemon rind and juice, the water, remaining sugar, and butter. Over a moderate heat, bring the mixture to the boil. Whisk in the eggs and cornflour, and return to the boil. Whisk until thick, for about 5 minutes. Remove from the heat. Cover with greaseproof paper to stop a skin forming and set aside. For the icing, cream the butter and icing sugar until smooth. Stir in the lemon rind and enough lemon juice to obtain a thick, spreadable consistency.

Sandwich the three cake layers with the lemon custard mixture. Spread the icing over the top and sides. Cover the cake all over with the shredded coconut, pressing it in gently.

BANANA AND LEMON CAKE

Light, moist and flavoursome, this cake keeps very well and is everybody's favourite.

Serves 8-10

250g/9oz/2¼ cups plain flour

6.5ml/1¼ tsp baking powder

pinch of salt

115g/4oz/½ cup unsalted butter, at
*   room temperature*

200g/7oz/scant 1 cup caster sugar

75g/3oz/½ cup soft light brown sugar

2 eggs

2.5ml/½ tsp grated lemon rind

225g/8oz/1 cup mashed, very
*   ripe bananas*

5ml/1 tsp vanilla essence

60ml/4 tbsp milk

75g/3oz/¾ cup chopped walnuts

lemon-rind curls, to decorate

For the icing

115g/4oz/½ cup butter, at
*   room temperature*

450g/1lb/4½ cups icing sugar

5ml/1 tsp grated lemon rind

45–75ml/3–5 tbsp lemon juice

Preheat the oven to 180°C/350°F/Gas 4. Grease two 23cm/9in round cake tins and line the base of each with non-stick baking paper. Sift the flour, baking powder and salt into a bowl.

Beat the butter and sugars in a large mixing bowl until light and fluffy. Beat in the eggs, one at a time, then stir in the lemon rind.

Mix the mashed bananas with the vanilla essence and milk in a small bowl. Stir this, in batches, into the creamed butter mixture, alternating with the sifted flour. Stir lightly until just blended. Fold in the walnuts.

Divide the mixture between the cake tins and spread evenly. Bake for 30–35 minutes, until a skewer inserted in the centre comes out clean. Leave to stand for 5 minutes before turning out on to a wire rack. Peel off the lining paper and leave to cool.

Make the icing. Cream the butter in a bowl until smooth, then gradually beat in the icing sugar. Stir in the lemon rind and enough of the lemon juice to make a spreading consistency.

Place one of the cakes on a serving plate. Spread over one-third of the icing, then top with the second cake. Spread the remaining icing evenly over the top and sides of the cake. Decorate with lemon-rind curls.

SUMMER STRAWBERRY GATEAU

No one could resist the appeal of little heartsease pansies. This strawberry-filled cake would be lovely for a summer occasion in the garden.

Serves 6–8

100g/3¾oz/scant ½ cup soft margarine
100g/3¾oz/scant ½ cup caster sugar
10ml/2 tsp clear honey
150g/5oz/1¼ cups self-raising flour
2.5ml/½ tsp baking powder
30ml/2 tbsp milk
2 eggs, plus 1 egg white for crystallizing
15ml/1 tbsp rose water
15ml/1 tbsp Cointreau or
  orange liqueur
16 heartsease pansy flowers
caster sugar, for crystallizing
icing sugar, to decorate
450g/1lb/3 cups strawberries
strawberry leaves, to decorate

Preheat the oven to 190°C/375°F/Gas 5. Grease and lightly flour a ring mould. Put the soft margarine, sugar, honey, flour, baking powder, milk and 2 eggs into a mixing bowl and beat well for 1 minute. Add the rose water and Cointreau or orange liqueur and mix well.

Pour the mixture into the prepared tin and bake for 40 minutes, or until a skewer inserted in the centre comes out clean. Leave to stand for a few minutes and then turn out on to a wire rack and leave to cool.

Crystallize the pansies by painting them with lightly beaten egg white and sprinkling lightly with caster sugar. Leave to dry.

Transfer the cake to a serving plate and sift over a little icing sugar. Fill the centre of the ring with strawberries and decorate with crystallized pansies and strawberry leaves.

AMERICAN BERRY SHORTCAKE

This classic dessert can be assembled up to an hour in advance and kept chilled until required.

Serves 8

300ml/¹/₂ pint/1¹/₄ cups
whipping cream
25g/1oz/2 tbsp icing sugar, sifted
675g/1¹/₂lb/4 cups strawberries or
mixed berries, halved or sliced if large
50g/2oz/¹/₄ cup caster sugar, or to taste

For the shortcake
225g/8oz/2 cups plain flour
10ml/2 tsp baking powder
65g/2¹/₂oz/5 tbsp caster sugar
115g/4oz/¹/₂ cup butter
75ml/5 tbsp milk
1 size 1 egg

Preheat the oven to 230°C/450°F/Gas 8. Grease a 20cm/8in round cake tin. To make the shortcake, sift the flour, baking powder and sugar into a bowl. Add the butter and rub in until the mixture resembles fine crumbs. Combine the milk and egg. Add to the crumb mixture and stir just until evenly mixed to a soft dough.

Put the dough in the prepared tin and pat out to an even layer. Bake for 15–20 minutes or until a wooden skewer inserted in the centre comes out clean. Leave to cool slightly.

Whip the cream until it starts to thicken. Add the icing sugar and continue whipping until the cream will hold soft peaks.

Put the berries in a bowl. Sprinkle with the caster sugar and toss together lightly. Cover and set aside for the berries to give up some juice.

Remove the cooled shortcake from the tin. With a long, serrated knife, split the shortcake horizontally into two equal layers.

Put the bottom layer on a serving plate. Top with half of the berries and most of the cream. Set the second layer on top and press down gently. Spoon the remaining berries over the top layer (or serve them separately) and add the remaining cream in small, decorative dollops.

CRANBERRY AND APPLE RING

Tangy cranberries add an unusual flavour to this light-textured cake. It is best eaten very fresh.

Serves 4–6

225g/8oz/2 cups self-raising flour
5ml/1 tsp ground cinnamon
90ml/6 tbsp light muscovado sugar
1 crisp eating apple, cored and diced
75g/3oz/⅔ cup fresh or frozen
  cranberries
60ml/4 tbsp sunflower oil
150ml/¾ pint/⅔ cup apple juice
cranberry jelly and apple slices,
  to decorate

Preheat the oven to 180°C/350°F/Gas 4. Lightly grease a 1 litre/1¼ pint/ 4 cup ring tin with oil. It is easiest to do this with a pastry brush, or you could use a piece of kitchen paper.

Sift together the flour and ground cinnamon, then stir in the sugar. Toss together the diced apple and cranberries. Stir the fruit into the dry ingredients, then add the sunflower oil and apple juice and beat well until thoroughly combined.

Spoon the cake mixture into the prepared ring tin and bake in the preheated oven for about 35–40 minutes, or until the cake is firm to the touch. Turn the cake out and leave it to cool on a wire cooling rack.

Just before serving, warm the cranberry jelly in a small saucepan over a gentle heat. Decorate the top of the ring with the prepared apple slices, then drizzle the warmed cranberry jelly over the apple pieces, letting it run down the sides of the ring.

COOK'S TIP
Fresh cranberries are now
readily available throughout the
winter months and if you don't
use them all at once, they can be
frozen for up to a year.

APPLE CRUMBLE CAKE

A rich and filling cake which is excellent served with thick cream or custard.

Serves 8–10

For the topping

75g/3oz/³/4 cup self-raising flour

2.5ml/¹/2 tsp ground cinnamon

40g/1¹/2oz/3 tbsp butter

30ml/2 tbsp caster sugar

For the base

50g/2oz/4 tbsp butter, softened

90ml/6 tbsp caster sugar

1 egg, beaten

115g/4oz/1 cup self-raising
  flour, sifted

2 cooking apples (about 450g/1lb),
  peeled, cored and sliced

50g/2oz/¹/3 cup sultanas

To decorate

1 red eating apple, cored, thinly sliced
  and tossed in lemon juice

30ml/2 tbsp caster sugar, sifted

pinch of ground cinnamon

Preheat the oven to 180°C/350°F/Gas 4. Lightly grease and line a deep 18cm/7in springform tin.

To make the topping, sift the flour and cinnamon together into a bowl. Rub in the butter until the mixture forms soft crumbs, then stir in the sugar. Set aside until needed.

To make the base for the cake, put the butter, sugar, egg and flour into a bowl and beat for 1–2 minutes until smooth. Spoon into the prepared tin and even out the surface.

Mix together the apple slices and sultanas and spread them evenly over the top of the base. Sprinkle with the topping.

Bake in the centre of the preheated oven for about 1 hour. Then remove from the oven and cool in the tin for 10 minutes before turning out on to a wire cooling rack and peeling off the lining paper. Serve warm or cool, decorated with the prepared slices of red eating apple and with caster sugar and cinnamon sprinkled over the top.

WARM LEMON AND SYRUP CAKE

After soaking in a tangy lemon syrup, this cake is both delightfully sweet and tart.

Serves 8

3 eggs

175g/6oz/³/4 cup butter, softened

175g/6oz/³/4 cup caster sugar

175g/6oz/1¹/2 cups self-raising flour

50g/2oz/¹/2 cup ground almonds

1.5ml/¹/4 tsp freshly grated nutmeg

50g/2oz candied lemon peel, finely chopped

grated rind of 1 lemon

30ml/2 tbsp lemon juice

poached pears, to serve

For the syrup

175g/6oz/³/4 cup caster sugar

juice of 3 lemons

Preheat the oven to 180°C/350°F/Gas 4. Grease and line the base of a deep, round 20cm/8in cake tin.

Place all the cake ingredients in a large bowl and beat well for 2–3 minutes, until light and fluffy.

Tip the mixture into the prepared tin, spread level and bake for 1 hour, or until golden and firm to the touch.

Meanwhile, make the syrup. Put the sugar, lemon juice and 75ml/5 tbsp water in a pan. Heat gently, stirring until the sugar has dissolved, then boil, without stirring, for 1–2 minutes.

Turn out the cake on to a plate with a rim. Prick the surface of the cake all  over with a fork, then pour over the hot syrup. Leave to soak for about 30 minutes. Serve the cake warm with thin wedges of poached pears.

CHOCOLATE CAKE WITH BANANA SAUCE

Caramelized banana and rum sauce tastes superb with wedges of chocolate cake.

Serves 6

*115g/4oz plain chocolate, broken
    into squares*
*115g/4oz/½ cup unsalted butter, at
    room temperature*
15ml/1 tbsp instant coffee powder
5 eggs, separated
225g/8oz/1 cup granulated sugar
115g/4oz/1 cup plain flour
5ml/1 tsp ground cinnamon

For the sauce

4 ripe bananas
60ml/4 tbsp soft light brown sugar
15ml/1 tbsp lemon juice
175ml/6fl oz/¾ cup whipping cream
15ml/1 tbsp rum (optional)

Preheat the oven to 180°C/350°F/Gas 4. Grease a 20cm/8in round cake tin. Bring a small saucepan of water to the boil. Remove it from the heat and place a heatproof bowl on top. Add the chocolate and butter to the bowl and leave until melted, stirring occasionally. Stir in the coffee powder and set aside.

Mix the egg yolks and granulated sugar in a bowl. Beat by hand or with an electric mixer until thick and lemon-coloured. Add the chocolate mixture and beat on low speed for just long enough to blend the mixtures evenly.

Sift the flour and cinnamon into a bowl. In another bowl, beat the egg whites to stiff peaks. Fold a spoon of egg white into the chocolate mixture to lighten it. Fold in the remaining egg white in batches, alternating with the sifted flour mixture.

Pour the mixture into the prepared tin. Bake for 40–50 minutes or until a skewer inserted in the centre comes out clean. Turn out on to a wire rack.

Preheat the grill. Make the sauce. Slice the bananas into a shallow, flameproof dish. Add the brown sugar and lemon juice and stir to mix. Place under the grill and cook, stirring occasionally, for about 8 minutes until the sugar is caramelized and bubbling. Mash the bananas into the sauce until almost smooth. Stir in the cream and rum, if using. Slice the cake and serve it warm, with the sauce.

PINEAPPLE AND GINGER CAKE

This tasty cake is packed with flavours; apricot and pineapple are combined with tangy orange and lemon and spiked with the refreshing, peppery taste of ginger.

Serves 10–12

175g/6oz/³/4 cup unsalted butter

150g/5oz/³/4 cup caster sugar

3 eggs, beaten

few drops vanilla essence

225g/8oz/2 cups plain flour, sifted

1.5ml/¼ tsp salt

7.5ml/1½ tsp baking powder

225g/8oz/1¹/3 cups ready-to-eat dried apricots, chopped

115g/4oz/½ cup each chopped crystallized ginger and crystallized pineapple

grated rind and juice of ½ orange

grated rind and juice of ½ lemon

a little milk

Preheat the oven to 180°C/350°F/Gas 4. Double line a 20cm/8in round or 18cm/7in square cake tin. Cream the butter and sugar together until the mixture is light and fluffy.

Gradually beat the eggs into the creamed mixture with the vanilla essence, beating well after each addition. Sift together the flour, salt and baking powder into a bowl, and add a little to the mixture with the last of the egg, then fold in the rest.

Fold in the fruit, ginger and fruit rinds gently, then add sufficient fruit juice and milk to give a fairly soft dropping consistency.

Spoon into the prepared tin and smooth the top with a wet spoon. Bake for 20 minutes, then reduce the oven temperature to 160°C/325°F/Gas 3 for a further 1½–2 hours, or until firm to the touch and a skewer comes out of the centre clean.

Leave the cake to cool in the tin, then turn out and wrap in fresh paper before storing in an airtight tin

COOK'S TIP

This is not a long-keeping cake, but it does freeze, well-wrapped in greaseproof paper and then overwrapped in foil.

BANANA NUT BREAD

Banana bread is always popular. This delicious, healthy version has added pecan nuts.

Makes 1 loaf

*115g/4oz/½ cup unsalted butter, at
  room temperature*

115g/4oz/½ cup granulated sugar

2 eggs, at room temperature

115g/4oz/1 cup plain flour

5ml/1 tsp bicarbonate of soda

1.5ml/¼ tsp salt

5ml/1 tsp ground cinnamon

50g/2oz/½ cup wholemeal flour

3 large ripe bananas

5ml/1 tsp vanilla essence

50g/2oz/½ cup pecan nuts, chopped

COOK'S TIP
*If the cake mixture shows signs
of curdling when you add the
eggs, beat in a little of the sifted
flour mixture.*

Preheat the oven to 180°C/350°F/Gas 4. Line the bottom and sides of a 23 x 13cm/9 x 5in loaf tin with non-stick baking paper.

Using an electric mixer, cream the butter and sugar in a bowl until light and fluffy. Add the eggs, one at a time, beating well after each addition.

Sift the plain flour, bicarbonate of soda, salt and cinnamon over the butter mixture. Stir in thoroughly, then stir in the wholemeal flour.

Mash the bananas to a purée and stir into the mixture. Stir in the vanilla essence and pecan nuts. Pour into the prepared tin and level the surface.

Bake the loaf for 50–60 minutes, until a skewer inserted in the centre comes out clean. Turn out on to a wire rack to cool.

ORANGE HONEY BREAD

Honey improves the keeping quality of cakes and breads, but this is so delicious that you are unlikely to be able to put the theory to the test.

Makes 1 loaf
275g/10oz/2½ cups plain flour
12.5ml/2½ tsp baking powder
2.5ml/½ tsp bicarbonate of soda
2.5ml/½ tsp salt
25g/1oz/2 tbsp margarine
250ml/8fl oz/1 cup clear honey
1 egg, lightly beaten
20ml/4 tbsp grated orange rind
175ml/6fl oz/¾ cup fresh
*   orange juice*
75g/3oz/¾ cup chopped walnuts

Preheat the oven to 160°C/325°F/Gas 3. Grease a 23 x 13cm/9 x 5in loaf tin and line the base with non-stick baking paper. Sift the flour, baking powder, bicarbonate of soda and salt together.

Cream the margarine in a mixing bowl until soft. Stir in the honey until well mixed, then stir in the lightly beaten egg. Add the orange rind and stir to combine thoroughly.

Fold the flour mixture into the honey and egg mixture in three batches, alternating with the orange juice. Stir in the walnuts.

Pour into the prepared tin and bake for about 1 hour, or until a cake tester inserted in the centre of the loaf comes out clean. Leave to stand for 10 minutes before turning out on to a wire rack to cool.

BANANA GINGER PARKIN

Bananas and ginger make a winning combination. This parkin actually improves with keeping.

Makes 12 bars

200g/7oz/1¾ cups plain flour

10ml/2 tsp bicarbonate of soda

10ml/2 tsp ground ginger

150g/5oz/1¾ cups medium oatmeal

60ml/4 tbsp dark muscovado sugar

75g/3oz/6 tbsp butter or margarine

150g/5oz/⅔ cup golden syrup

1 egg, beaten

3 ripe bananas, mashed

75g/3oz/¾ cup icing sugar

stem ginger, to decorate

COOK'S TIP
This is a nutritious, energy-giving cake that is an excellent choice for packed lunches, as it does not break up or crumble very easily.

Preheat the oven to 160°C/325°F/Gas 3. Grease and line a 28 x 18cm/11 x 7in cake tin. Sift the flour, bicarbonate of soda and ginger into a bowl, then stir in the oatmeal.

Melt the sugar, butter or margarine and syrup in a saucepan, then stir into the flour mixture. Beat in the egg and mashed bananas.

Spoon the mixture into the tin and bake for about 1 hour, or until firm to the touch. Allow to cool in the tin, then turn out and cut into bars.

Sift the icing sugar into a bowl and stir in just enough water to make a smooth, runny icing. Drizzle the icing over each square and top the parkin with slices of stem ginger.

BANANA MUFFINS

Make plenty of these delectable treats – banana muffins are irresistible at any time of the day.

Makes 10

225g/8oz/2 cups plain flour

5ml/1 tsp baking powder

5ml/1 tsp bicarbonate of soda

1.5ml/¼ tsp salt

1.5ml/¼ tsp grated nutmeg

2.5ml/½ tsp ground cinnamon

3 large ripe bananas

1 egg

50g/2oz/⅓ cup soft dark
 brown sugar

60ml/4 tbsp vegetable oil

40g/1½oz/¼ cup raisins

Preheat the oven to 190°C/375°F/Gas 5. Line 10 muffin cups with paper liners or grease them lightly. Sift the flour, baking powder, bicarbonate of soda, salt, nutmeg and cinnamon into a bowl. Set aside.

Mash the bananas in a mixing bowl until creamy. Using a hand-held electric mixer, beat in the egg, sugar and oil. Add the dry ingredients and mix until just blended. Stir in the raisins.

Fill the muffin cups two-thirds full. Bake for 20–25 minutes or until the tops spring back when lightly touched. Transfer the muffins to a wire rack to cool slightly. Serve warm.

COOK'S TIP

If there are any empty cups in the muffin tray when you have used up the mixture, fill them with water before placing the tray in the oven to ensure that the muffins bake evenly.

CHOCOLATE AND BANANA BROWNIES

Bananas give brownies a delicious flavour and keep them marvellously moist.

Makes 9

75ml/5 tbsp cocoa powder

15ml/1 tbsp caster sugar

75ml/5 tbsp milk

3 large bananas, mashed

175g/6oz/1 cup soft light
*   brown sugar*

5ml/1 tsp vanilla essence

5 egg whites

75g/3oz/³⁄₄ cup self-raising flour

50g/2oz/²⁄₃ cup oat bran

15ml/1 tbsp icing sugar, for dusting

COOK'S TIP

Store these brownies in an
airtight container for one day
before eating them – their
flavour becomes stronger and
improves with keeping.

Preheat the oven to 180°C/350°F/Gas 4. Line a 20cm/8in square baking tin with non-stick baking paper. In a bowl, mix the cocoa powder and caster sugar with the milk. Add the bananas, brown sugar and vanilla essence. Mix well.

In a mixing bowl, beat the egg whites lightly with a fork. Add the chocolate mixture and continue to beat well. Sift the flour over the mixture and fold in with the oat bran. Pour into the prepared tin.

Bake for 40 minutes or until firm. Cool in the tin for 10 minutes, then turn out on to a wire rack and cool completely. Cut into nine wedges and dust lightly with icing sugar before serving.

LEMON SPICE BISCUITS

The crisp biscuits are perfect for most occasions and are delicious served with ice cream.

Makes 50

240g/8¹/₂oz/2¹/₈ cups plain flour

2.5ml/¹/₂ tsp salt

10ml/2 tsp ground cinnamon

225g/8oz/1 cup unsalted butter, at room temperature

200g/7oz/1 cup sugar

2 eggs

5ml/1 tsp vanilla essence

grated rind of 1 lemon

In a bowl, sift together the flour, salt, and cinnamon. Set aside. Cream the butter and sugar and beat until the mixture is light and fluffy. Beat together the eggs and vanilla, then gradually stir into the butter mixture with the lemon rind. Stir in the flour mixture. Divide the dough into four parts, then roll each into 5cm/2in diameter logs. Wrap in foil and chill until firm. Preheat the oven to 190°C/375°F/Gas 5. Grease two baking sheets. Cut the dough into 5mm/¹/₄in slices. Place the rounds on the sheets and bake until lightly coloured, for about 10 minutes. Transfer to a wire rack to cool.

INDEX